1987

Tax Reform and the U.S. Economy

Brookings Dialogues on Public Policy

The presentations and discussions at Brookings conferences and seminars often deserve wide circulation as contributions to public understanding of issues of national importance. The Brookings Dialogues on Public Policy series is intended to make such statements and commentary available to a broad and general audience, usually in summary form. The series supplements the Institution's research publications by reflecting the contrasting, often lively, and sometimes conflicting views of elected and appointed government officials, other leaders in public and private life, and scholars. In keeping with their origin and purpose, the Dialogues are not subjected to the formal review procedures established for the Institution's research publications. Brookings publishes them in the belief that they are worthy of public consideration but does not assume responsibility for their accuracy or objectivity. And, as in all Brookings publications, the judgments, conclusions, and recommendations presented in the Dialogues should not be ascribed to the trustees, officers, or other staff members of the Brookings Institution.

Tax Reform
and the U.S. Economy

Papers by HENRY J. AARON
            LARRY L. DILDINE
            EUGENE STEUERLE
            PATRIC H. HENDERSHOTT, JAMES R. FOLLAIN
            & DAVID C. LING
            presented at a conference at the Brookings Institution,
            December 2, 1986

Edited by JOSEPH A. PECHMAN

THE BROOKINGS INSTITUTION
Washington, D.C.

About Brookings

THE BROOKINGS INSTITUTION is a private nonprofit organization devoted to research, education, and publication in economics, government, foreign policy, and the social sciences generally. Its principal purpose is to bring knowledge to bear on the current and emerging public policy problems facing the American people. In its research, Brookings functions as an independent analyst and critic, committed to publishing its findings for the information of the public. In its conferences and other activities, it serves as a bridge between scholarship and public policy, bringing new knowledge to the attention of decisionmakers and affording scholars a better insight into policy issues. Its activities are carried out through three research programs (Economic Studies, Governmental Studies, Foreign Policy Studies), a Center for Public Policy Education, a Publications Program, and a Social Science Computation Center.

The Institution was incorporated in 1927 to merge the Institute for Government Research, founded in 1916 as the first private organization devoted to public policy issues at the national level; the Institute of Economics, established in 1922 to study economic problems; and the Robert Brookings Graduate School of Economics and Government, organized in 1924 as a pioneering experiment in training for public service. The consolidated institution was named in honor of Robert Somers Brookings (1850–1932), a St. Louis businessman whose leadership shaped the earlier organizations.

Brookings is financed largely by endowment and by the support of philanthropic foundations, corporations, and private individuals. Its funds are devoted to carrying out its own research and educational activities. It also undertakes some unclassified government contract studies, reserving the right to publish its findings.

A Board of Trustees is responsible for general supervision of the Institution, approval of fields of investigation, and safeguarding the independence of the Institution's work. The President is the chief administrative officer, responsible for formulating and coordinating policies, recommending projects, approving publications, and selecting the staff.

Editor's Preface

PASSAGE of the Tax Reform Act of 1986 marks a new chapter in the history of income taxation. The act eliminated the investment tax credit, removed the tax advantages of most tax shelters, equalized the tax rates on capital gains and ordinary income, and strengthened the minimum taxes applying to individuals and corporations. The revenues raised by these and other base-broadening provisions were used to increase the personal exemptions and standard deductions and to reduce the corporate and individual income tax rates. Almost every household and business in the United States will be affected by this legislation.

This volume in the series of Brookings Dialogues on Public Policy reports on the proceedings of a conference to evaluate the economic effects of the 1986 tax reforms. The conference, held at the Brookings Institution on December 2, 1986, was organized by the Brookings Center for Public Policy Education. The participants included key staff members of the congressional tax-writing committees, former and present officials of the Treasury Department, leading economists and tax lawyers, and representatives of the business community. The opinions expressed by the participants reflect their own views and not those of the organizations with which they are affiliated.

Walter E. Beach organized the conference with the assistance of Joan P. Milan, and Nancy Davidson and James Schneider edited the manuscript.

The Brookings Institution is grateful to the authors and discussants of the papers and to the experts who attended the conference. We believe that their views, which are summarized in the volume, will improve public understanding of the 1986 legislation.

Joseph A. Pechman

February 1987
Washington, D.C.

Contents

ix

Introduction

JOSEPH A. PECHMAN

THE Tax Reform Act of 1986 is one of the most important pieces of tax legislation ever passed in the United States. After decades of erosion, the individual and corporation income taxes have been purged of numerous tax preferences and big loopholes have been plugged. The top individual income tax rates have been cut to their lowest levels since 1931, and the corporate rate has been reduced to the 1941 level. But the legislation is complicated and few people really understand the effects it may have on particular individuals, business firms, and the economy as a whole.

The papers and discussions presented in this volume are intended to explain in nontechnical language the important provisions of the 1986 act and their economic effects. The first paper, by Henry J. Aaron, describes the major features of the bill, what its most important accomplishments were, and what opportunities were missed. Aaron believes that the act greatly improves the tax law, but a number of significant opportunities for further improvement were neglected. This is followed by Larry L. Dildine's analysis of the effect of the bill on American industry. The act was intended to reduce the influence of tax policy on the allocation of economic resources. Dildine shows in detail which industries will gain and which will lose from this reallocation. The next paper, by Eugene Steuerle, examines the effect of the new law on financial decisions. He argues that it will spur economic growth by encouraging more efficient investment. The most radical changes in the bill apply to real estate and housing; the final paper, by Patric H. Hendershott, James R. Follain, and David C. Ling, estimates the effect of these changes on rents, market values, and homeownership.

Solid gains and neglected opportunities

The most important elements of reform in the act were, according to Aaron, the increase in the personal exemption and the standard deduction, the increase in the earned income credit, the reductions in the top marginal individual income tax rate from 50 percent to

1

28 percent and in the general corporate tax rate from 46 percent to 34 percent, and the broadening of the tax base by repealing numerous special provisions, particularly the capital gains preference. Repeal of the investment credit and revisions in the depreciation schedules will result in more equal treatment of various types of assets and different industries. And the overall progression in the tax system will be increased both by the removal of 6 million people from the tax rolls and by the shift of about $24 billion in taxes a year from individuals to corporations.

Aaron believes that the two major accomplishments of the act were the reduction of the marginal tax rates and the narrowing of the tax differentials among different assets and industries. The marginal rate reductions will allow people to keep more of each additional dollar of income and thus will increase incentives to work and to save. The best estimates suggest that work effort will increase by perhaps 1 percent, but the effect on saving is difficult to measure. The more uniform treatment of business investments, as well as the elimination of the capital gains preference, will promote more efficient use of capital by U.S. industry.

Although the 1986 act has been criticized by some for increasing the cost of capital, Aaron points out that the effect of the reduced incentive to invest will tend to be offset by the increased efficiency in the use of capital. Moreover, any reduction in investment that might occur could be offset by other measures. For example, according to some models, a reduction of 0.8 percent in interest rates would offset the effect of the increase in the cost of capital.

High up on Aaron's list of missed opportunities was the failure to adjust capital income for inflation. In the U.S. tax system, an asset yielding 10 percent in nominal terms but only 5 percent after inflation would be subject to tax on the full 10 percent, even though the real rate of return is only 5 percent. To cushion the effect of this distortion in the measurement of income, Congress enacted numerous ad hoc provisions over the years that contributed to public disillusionment over the fairness of the tax system. Aaron warns that inflation can undermine a tax system and urges that serious consideration be given to indexing the tax base at an early date.

Aaron also deplores the failure of Congress to make any progress in two other areas: the taxation of fringe benefits and the double taxation of dividends. He points out that it is unwise and unfair to encourage employers to provide tax-free benefits to their employees. He also believes that the tax law should not discriminate against equity financing and that some method of integrating the individual and corporation income taxes should be adopted to alleviate this problem.

On balance, Aaron believes that the effect of the act on economic performance will be small. Since disposable personal income will be increased, consumption is likely to be encouraged. There may be a reduction in investment, but the efficiency of investment will be improved by the elimination of tax shelters and other tax provisions favoring particular industries.

Impact on American industry

The official revenue estimates indicate that the new law will be "revenue neutral" over a period of five years. According to these estimates, individuals will receive a net tax cut of $120.5 billion in 1987–91, but this will be offset by a tax increase of $120.3 billion on corporations. Larry Dildine points out that the tax reduction for individuals conceals rather large tax increases on unincorporated business activities, while most of the corporate tax increase is concentrated in particular industries and does not apply to the corporate sector as a whole.

However, Dildine questions whether the new law will in fact be revenue neutral. He points out that the accounting changes and new minimum tax will produce most of their revenue in the first five years and the depreciation revisions will produce less additional revenue after 1991. Consequently, the new law may lose revenue over the long run.

According to Dildine, almost three-fifths of the corporate tax increase will come from revisions that will remove tax preferences of particular industries and increase the corporate minimum tax. The remainder is from provisions that are broadly applicable to corporations of all kinds. This "general" tax increase is the net result of tax increases from the repeal of the investment credit, changes in depreciation allowances, uniform accounting rules for investors, a new limitation on deductions for meals, travel, and entertainment, and a cutback of the dividend-received deduction for corporations, offset by the across-the-board cut in the corporate tax rate and increased credit for research and development expenses.

Less well known is the large accompanying tax increase on unincorporated business. Dildine points out that the limitations on tax shelters, repeal of the investment credit, the new minimum tax on individuals, and other structural changes are estimated to increase the tax on noncorporate business by $90 billion over the five-year period. This, he estimates, will be offset by about $40 billion of rate cuts, leaving a net additional tax on such businesses of about $50 billion at the individual level.

One of the key features of the new law is the change in the relative tax treatment of corporations compared with that of individual investors. First, the corporate tax rate will exceed the top-bracket individual income tax rate for the first time since the individual income tax was enacted in 1913. Second, capital gains will be taxed in full at the individual level. Third, "passive losses" will be deductible only against "passive income" at the individual level. These changes will encourage investors to move assets between sectors to achieve better matchups of incomes and deductions. Tax shelters in real estate, equipment leasing, and other activities can be expected to move to corporations, while growing businesses will get much better treatment if organized as partnerships.

Dildine believes that the new tax law will increase the tax burden on equipment-intensive industries and reduce it in other industries. Industries investing a large share of their earnings in machinery and equipment (such as steel, aluminum, and public utilities) will have higher capital costs as a result of the repeal of the investment credit and the reduction in depreciation allowances. The "high-tech" industries will benefit from the retention of the credit for research and development expenses and the corporate rate cut. Mature industries that require relatively little new investment to maintain productive capacity (such as the food, beverage, apparel, and service industries) will also pay lower taxes.

U.S.-based companies with operations in high-tax countries will not be able to credit as much of their foreign taxes against the reduced U.S. corporate tax. Some of these companies might find it profitable to bring back their foreign earnings to the United States. On the other hand, foreign-based multinationals with manufacturing operations in the United States may be subject to higher U.S. taxes and may reduce their investment here. If the decline in foreign investment more than offsets the repatriation of earnings, the dollar will be weakened, U.S. exports will be encouraged, and imports will be discouraged.

Like Aaron, Dildine believes that there are a number of disappointments in the new tax law. He deplores the lack of congressional interest in equalizing the tax on corporate and noncorporate earnings, the retroactive effect of many of the structural changes, and the additional complexity introduced by the new minimum tax and the foreign tax credit limitations. On the other hand, two major accomplishments more than make up for these deficiencies. The first is the move toward more equality in the taxation of income among different assets and industries. The second is the reduction in corporate and individual tax rates, which reduces the effect of the remaining distortions.

Financial decisions

Eugene Steuerle begins his analysis by contrasting the older tax policies with the Tax Reform Act of 1986. Under the old law, growth was usually encouraged by tax reductions, including those designed to provide investment and saving incentives. However, once the country moved into a new era of rising public debt, this option became less viable. Furthermore, some of the special incentives actually generated negative tax rates (that is, subsidies), particularly for highly leveraged activities like real estate and leasing. The new law eliminates many of these incentives on the ground that they are either ineffective or generate distortions. The hope is that a broad base combined with low tax rates will promote economic growth by allowing the market, rather than the tax system, to allocate financial resources.

Steuerle believes that on balance the new tax system will be good for the economy. While it will not stop recessions (and was not intended to do so), it will improve efficiency in the use of human and capital resources over the long run. Individuals and businesses with productive ideas will have better access to loanable funds, because the use of these funds for tax shelters and other uneconomic activities will be curtailed, if not eliminated. The equalization of tax rates among different types of investments will also improve the access of new and growing enterprises to investment funds.

Steuerle also believes that the new tax law will simultaneously reduce the demand for borrowed capital and increase its supply, thus exerting downward pressure on interest rates. Under the old law, there were tremendous opportunities for taxpayers to lower their taxes through additional borrowing and shifting of assets. The new law will severely restrict this type of "tax arbitrage," partly by imposing complicated limits on the amount of interest that can be deducted on individual returns and restricting the deduction of losses from passive investments to the gains from such investments. Furthermore, since most savers and borrowers will be in the same tax bracket, additional lending and borrowing will not reduce aggregate tax collections, as such activity did under the old law.

Steuerle agrees with Dildine that the new differential between the corporate tax rate and the top individual income tax rate will encourage the conversion of corporations into limited partnerships. However, if the financial sector will be able to create efficient liquid markets for such partnership shares, Congress may well step in to prevent significant revenue losses from disincorporation.

Steuerle also identifies a number of significant weaknesses in the new tax law. There is still an incentive to merge to take advantage of loss offsets and to avoid the minimum tax. The limitation on the deduction of investment interest payments by individuals will encourage substitution of mortgage borrowing for other types of borrowing. Finally, Steuerle also deplores the failure to adjust capital income for inflation. Although the lower tax rates will reduce the inflation tax penalty, any future increase in inflation will again create disparities in the tax treatment of different types of assets and encourage Congress to make ad hoc changes that could restore the tax distortions of the 1970s and early 1980s.

Real estate without shelters

One of the key features of the Tax Reform Act of 1986 is its attack on real estate tax shelters. Patric Hendershott and associates explain the nature of this attack and how it will affect real estate. The act defines a new category of economic activity—called "passive" activity—which is segregated from other activities for tax purposes. An activity is passive if the taxpayer does not materially participate in it. (All rental activities are passive.) Losses of individuals, partnerships, trusts, and personal service corporations from passive activities may offset income from other passive activities, but not other income (such as wages, interest, and dividends). Passive losses not used in a particular year can be carried forward to offset passive income in future years.

The new law also extends the existing "at-risk" rules to real estate. The amount at risk in a particular venture is generally the sum of the equity funds initially invested by the taxpayer and the amount of debt for which the owner is personally liable. Losses in a particular property are limited to the amount at risk. In addition to the passive loss and the at-risk rules, depreciation for real estate is reduced and tax depreciation that exceeds straight-line depreciation over a forty-year period is made subject to the minimum tax.

According to Hendershott and associates, the new tax rules could affect real estate markets significantly. The probability that net losses from some projects will not be currently deductible could raise the return required by investors from real estate investments and thus discourage such investments. Another likely response is that investors in properties with passive losses will sell their holdings to other investors with passive gains. If this is done on a large scale, the passive loss rules would have relatively small effects on real estate markets.

The reduction in the tax benefits of real estate will tend to increase rents on residential and commercial properties. The amount of the increase depends on what will happen to interest rates. If interest rates remain unchanged, the rise in rents could be large. However, Hendershott and associates agree with Steuerle that interest rates will decline, and they assume a decline of 1 percentage point in their calculations. On this assumption, they estimate that residential rents are likely to increase by 10 to 15 percent and commercial rents by 5 to 10 percent. The rise in rents will occur sooner in fast-growing markets with normal vacancy rates. Thus Hendershott and associates expect that it will take four years in cities where housing is tight and as much as twelve years where vacancy rates are high.

The market value of existing residential and commercial property would remain unchanged if rents adjusted immediately to the new higher levels. But because the adjustment will take place over a period of years, market values must decline to bring the rate of return up to the going rate for such property. Hendershott and associates believe that the decline will not exceed 4 percent in fast-growing markets, but may be as high as 8 percent in slow-growing markets with substantial excess capacity.

Although the new law continues the deductions for mortgage interest on first and second residences, two of its features will affect the after-tax cost of owner-occupied housing. First, the deductions will be worth less because tax rates will be lower. Second, interest rates are likely to decline. Hendershott and associates estimate that, if interest rates decline by 1 percentage point, costs will decline about 10 percent for homeowners with incomes below $30,000, rise by 5 percent for those with incomes of about $130,000 or more, and not change significantly for others. Thus housing prices will be higher or remain unchanged for the bulk of the housing market. They may be lower only at the very high end of the market (say, housing selling for $250,000 or more), but Hendershott and associates believe that the decline will be modest. The combination of lower costs for most homeowners and higher rents for apartment dwellers could increase home-ownership by about 3 percentage points over the next ten or twenty years.

A final feature of the law that will affect the housing market is a new tax credit for low-income rental housing. In 1987 the annual value of the tax credit will be about 9 percent of the cost of construction, but it will rise if interest rates rise and fall if they decline. For low-income housing with tax-exempt financing, the annual value of the credit in 1987 declines to 4 percent. Investors will qualify for the credit only if they fulfill a variety of restrictions, including a requirement that the property is rented to a significant degree to the intended low-income population. Hendershott and associates believe that the credit will provide a significant incentive to increase the construction of such housing. But it is difficult to judge how much low-income housing will be stimulated by the new credit.

Conference
discussion

The conference participants generally supported the view that the Tax Reform Act of 1986 will improve the tax laws of the United States. They particularly approved of the provisions that remove the poor from the tax rolls, the broadening of the bases of the individual and corporate income taxes, and the reduction in tax rates. These changes will increase the perceived fairness of the tax system and encourage businessmen to invest in projects on the basis of their before-tax rates of return, rather than on the basis of after-tax yields. The reductions in the tax value of the remaining deductions and preferences will also lessen the importance of tax considerations in business decisions.

A major concern of some of the participants was the shift of tax burdens from individuals to corporations and the resulting increase in the costs of capital. Although much of the corporate tax increase will come from firms and industries formerly benefiting from tax preferences, several expressed the view that this was no time to discourage investment anywhere in the economy. They acknowledged that capital will be more efficiently allocated, but they were not persuaded by the economists at the conference that the increased efficiency will more than offset the effect of the increase in capital costs.

There was universal approval of the decision by Congress to adjust the personal exemptions, standard deductions, rate brackets, and the earned income credit phaseout range for inflation. There was also general agreement that, in principle, it would be better to index capital income rather than to continue to tax nominal incomes and permit deductions for nominal interest paid. However, it was recognized that it would not be easy to adjust the income tax base for inflation.

The failure of Congress to do something about the double taxation of corporate dividends was deplored by some of the conference participants and applauded by others. Proponents of integrating the individual and corporate income taxes argued that debt financing should not be encouraged at the expense of equity financing. However, several participants pointed out that corporate managers are at best lukewarm about dividend relief, especially when compared with other uses of revenues, such as rate reductions or accelerations of depreciation deductions. Dividend relief would also put pressure on corporations to increase dividend payments and thus reduce the earnings retained for investment purposes. These participants saw little reason to sacrifice revenues in order to satisfy a principle that business did not support.

In this connection, it was pointed out that the discrepancy between the corporate tax rate and top individual income tax rate would encourage some businesses to disincorporate. If done on a large scale, disincorporation would automatically reduce the double taxation problem. A number of participants objected to the use of the tax system as a device to encourage one form of legal organization for business over another. None of the participants was willing to predict whether Congress will ultimately remove the differential between the top individual and corporate rates or place restrictions on the option to disincorporate.

Financial markets seem to have reacted favorably to the new tax law, even though the capital gains rate was increased. Several of the participants attributed this development to the reductions in tax rates on other incomes, particularly executive salaries, interest, and dividends. Moreover, the reduction in the tax rates on short-term gains—formerly taxed at rates up to 50 percent and now taxed at a maximum rate of 33 percent—may increase the volume of transactions. The reduction in tax arbitraging and the elimination of most of the advantages of real estate tax shelters were also expected to improve the allocation of financial resources.

The reservation about the bill expressed most frequently is its effect on compliance and administration. The new law is a distinct simplification for the 6 million taxpayers taken off the rolls altogether and the additional millions of low- and middle-income taxpayers who will no longer itemize. However, for high-income taxpayers and many corporations, the act introduced many provisions that will complicate business planning (for example, the minimum tax and the passive loss and interest limitations) and make compliance more difficult.

The Impossible Dream Comes True

HENRY J. AARON

LIKE the bewitched princess who watched endless suitors perish in the dragon's fire, advocates of tax equity and efficiency have despaired for decades as the occasional brave politician marched off on a futile quest for tax reform. In 1986, to almost universal surprise, the spell was broken. A bipartisan coalition of members of Congress and the president slew a host of political dragons and enacted a major tax overhaul that deserves to be honored as reform.

Any assessment of this landmark reform must address several broad questions: What was accomplished? What retrograde steps were mistakenly taken? What opportunities were missed? And how will the new tax law influence economic behavior?

To begin with, one should be clear on what the 1986 tax reform law is *not*. It is not a revolution of the American tax system in the sense that the introduction of a value-added tax or integration of the personal and corporate income taxes would be. It does not inaugurate a new era of simplicity. Nor will it launch the American economy into a new era of economic growth. It has not purged the tax system of distortions and illogic.

But the Tax Reform Act of 1986 stands as the most important improvement in the broad-based taxes on individual and corporate income in at least two decades. It deals in a fundamental way with many parts of the tax code that created widespread opportunities to avoid taxation and distorted the flow of investment into wasteful uses. By curtailing these provisions, the act makes possible a major reduction in statutory rates without loss of revenue or any decline in progressivity. Of the three stated goals of tax reform—increased economic efficiency and growth, fairness, and simplicity—the new law achieves major advances on the first and second and, on balance, modestly improves the third.

Elements of the reform

The most important elements of the reform are as follows.

—Personal exemptions are increased from $1,080 in 1986 to

10

$1,900 in 1987, $1,950 in 1988, and $2,000 in 1989, and the standard deduction is raised from $3,670 to $5,000 for couples and from $2,480 to $3,000 for single persons in 1988. The earned income tax credit is increased to 14 percent of earnings up to $5,714 (a maximum credit of $800 in 1987) and will be phased out, starting in 1988, on income above $9,000 a year. The ceiling and the starting point for the phaseout will be indexed for inflation. These changes boost the amount of income a family of four can receive before having to pay personal income tax from $9,574 in 1986 to $14,480 in 1988.

—The nominal personal tax rate schedule that ran from 11 percent to 50 percent is replaced by two rates: 15 percent, applicable to taxable incomes of $17,850 or less for single persons and $29,750 or less for joint filers, and 28 percent. For a four-person family claiming the standard deduction, the 28 percent bracket applies in 1988 to incomes over $42,550 ($29,750 plus $7,800 in personal exemptions and $5,000 in standard deductions). The top effective rate is not 28 percent but 33 percent because a number of advantages accorded to low-income taxpayers are recaptured from high-income taxpayers. These advantages include the taxation of some income at 15 percent and the privilege of taking personal exemptions. The maximum corporate income tax rate drops from 46 percent on profits over $100,000 to 34 percent on profits over $75,000.

—The tax base is broadened, most notably by provisions that reduce incentives for tax shelter investments and by the repeal of numerous special business deductions. The result is that both individual and corporate income tax rates can be cut with no loss of revenue.

—Discrepancies among tax rates on various types of investment are reduced by repeal of the investment tax credit, revision of depreciation deductions, and a variety of other provisions.

—The exclusion from taxation of 60 percent of long-term capital gains has been repealed, thereby reducing incentives to convert fully taxable ordinary income into long-term capital gains.

What was accomplished? The achievements of the Tax Reform Act of 1986 are significant in several important respects. First, the act reduces marginal tax rates for most taxpayers, although not all groups are equally affected. Of households with incomes below $20,000 a year, nearly 30 percent will face higher marginal tax rates, but the increased personal exemptions and standard deductions assure that fewer than 10 percent will actually pay more tax (see table 1).

Table 1. *Changes in Taxes under 1986 Reform for All Taxpayers*[a]
Percent unless otherwise indicated

Gross income bracket (dollars)	Marginal tax rates			Total personal taxes			Total returns (thousands)
	Reduced	Unchanged[b]	Increased	Reduced	Unchanged[b]	Increased	
Under 10,000	17.2	55.2	27.6	46.8	50.4	2.9	29,468
10,000–19,999	57.3	11.5	31.2	72.9	15.2	11.9	24,718
20,000–39,999	81.8	1.9	16.3	70.7	15.2	14.1	30,230
40,000–49,999	54.6	1.7	43.8	73.4	17.5	9.1	9,022
50,000 and over	87.2	0.7	12.1	60.2	21.7	18.1	14,434
All taxpayers	57.0	18.5	24.6	63.5	25.9	10.7	107,872

Source: Brookings tax model developed by senior research programmer Chuck Byce.
a. Based on projected levels of income in 1988; figures are rounded.
b. Includes change in taxes of less than 5 percent or less than $50.

Table 2. *Changes in Marginal Tax Rates, by Number of Earners*[a]
Percent unless otherwise indicated

Gross income bracket (dollars)	One earner or none				Two earners			
	Reduced	Unchanged[b]	Increased	Total returns (thousands)	Reduced	Unchanged[b]	Increased	Total returns (thousands)
Under 10,000	17.1	54.9	28.1	28,971	25.0	71.8	3.2	496
10,000–19,999	60.7	12.0	27.3	22,559	21.7	6.3	72.0	2,159
20,000–39,999	77.5	2.6	19.9	20,891	91.3	0.4	8.3	9,340
40,000–49,999	64.9	3.4	31.6	4,336	45.0	0	55.0	4,686
50,000 and over	87.8	1.3	10.8	6,369	86.8	0.2	13.0	8,064
Total	52.0	23.3	24.7	83,126	73.7	2.2	24.1	24,745

Source: See table 1.
a. Based on projected levels of income in 1988; figures are rounded.
b. Includes change in taxes of less than 5 percent or less than $50.

Table 3. *Changes in Marginal Tax Rates for Itemizers and Nonitemizers*[a]
Percent unless otherwise indicated

Gross income bracket (dollars)	Itemizers				Nonitemizers			
	Reduced	Unchanged[b]	Increased	Total returns (thousands)	Reduced	Unchanged[b]	Increased	Total returns (thousands)
Under 10,000	40.5	37.7	21.6	1,455	16.0	56.1	28.0	28,013
10,000–19,999	42.4	15.5	42.2	3,069	59.4	10.9	29.7	21,648
20,000–39,999	79.3	3.3	17.5	12,295	83.5	1.0	15.5	17,935
40,000–49,999	55.6	2.0	42.4	6,357	52.2	0.9	46.9	2,665
50,000 and over	86.9	0.7	12.4	12,600	89.5	0.7	9.7	1,834
Total	73.0	4.6	22.4	35,776	49.0	25.4	25.6	72,095

Source: See table 1.
a. Based on projected levels of income in 1988; figures are rounded.
b. Includes change in taxes of less than 5 percent or less than $50.

Marginal tax rates will be reduced for nearly 90 percent of households with incomes of $50,000 a year or more, but because these taxpayers are hit hard by base-broadening reforms, only three in five of those households will pay less tax. Taxable units with two earners are more likely than units with one earner or none to experience reduced marginal tax rates because two-earner households tend to have high incomes (see table 2). The same reason explains why marginal rates are likely to go down more for taxable units that itemize their deductions than for units that take the standard deduction (see table 3).

Because most people will be able to keep more of each additional dollar that they can earn from work, the labor supply is likely to increase. Because not all marginal rates go down and most changes are small, the effect on labor supply will not be dramatic—a 1 percent increase in hours, according to estimates made by Jerry Hausman and James Poterba.[1] But that would be enough to increase productive capacity about $35 billion a year in 1986 prices.

Second, the 1986 act restores to the tax system some of the progressivity lost through inflation and recent legislation. The increases in the personal exemption and the standard deduction and the liberalization of the earned income tax credit directly remove approximately 6 million low-income taxpayers from the tax rolls. These provisions are responsible for the large percentage reductions in tax liabilities of taxpayers with income below $20,000.

Congressional staff estimates indicate that all income classes enjoy cuts in *personal* income taxes, reflecting the shift of approximately $24 billion in taxes each year from individuals to corporations. But the increased corporate income taxes also impose burdens on the people who own capital by reducing their after-tax return on assets. If one takes account of both personal and corporate tax burdens, not all income brackets gain, because the plan is revenue neutral. The resulting pattern is clearly progressive, with taxpayers in income brackets below $50,000 a year enjoying reductions and taxpayers in income brackets above $50,000 a year bearing increases (see table 4).

The third major accomplishment will be an increase in the efficiency of investment. Previous tax law favored certain kinds of investments over others in two ways. First, it imposed highly unequal rates on different assets and industries, which favored

---

1. Jerry A. Hausman and James M. Poterba, "Household Behavior and the Tax Reform Act of 1986," *Journal of Economic Perspectives,* forthcoming.

Table 4. *Estimated Change in Tax Burdens in 1988, by Income Brackets*

Income class (dollars)	Change in personal income and corporate income tax burdens (percent)[a]	Change in total tax burdens (percent)[b]
Under 10,000	−32.0	−12.5
10,000–20,000	−8.1	−3.1
20,000–30,000	−4.1	−1.8
30,000–40,000	−4.1	−2.0
40,000–50,000	−6.1	−3.1
50,000–70,000	+0.7	+0.4
70,000–100,000	+5.3	+3.9
100,000–200,000	+6.0	+5.0
200,000 and above	+9.2	+8.2

Source: Author's estimates.

a. Change in personal and corporate income tax burdens divided by prior personal and corporate income tax burdens, divided by 100.

b. Change in personal and corporate income tax burdens divided by prior total tax burdens, times 100. Total tax burdens include, in addition to income taxes, payroll and excise taxes.

lightly taxed but low-productivity investment over heavily taxed investment that might be more productive. This distortion hindered growth in output. Second, the previous law contained a variety of provisions that made tax shelters possible. Shelters worked especially well for investments in assets that are good collateral for loans and can be traded with low transaction costs, such as commercial real estate, multifamily housing, airplanes, and railroad cars.

The tax reform act takes large steps to reduce these distortions. The repeal of the investment tax credit and revisions in depreciation schedules narrow the range of effective corporate income tax rates on various assets and industries (see table 5). And the new law erects formidable roadblocks to tax shelters; in addition to repealing the investment tax credit and stretching out depreciation deductions on structures, the reform law curtails deductibility of investment interest, limits the deductibility of losses on passive investments (defined as all real estate investments and other projects the investor does not actively manage), and strengthens the minimum tax to ensure that most taxpayers will pay some tax.

The tax reform law also repeals the exclusion of 60 percent of long-term capital gains. Congress has taxed only a portion of such gains because it feared that realization of large gains could subject individuals to high marginal rates in the year of realization and, in recent years, because part of many capital gains has been the illusory result of inflation. Congress also hoped that low tax

Table 5. *Effective Tax Rates, by Asset Type and Industry*
Percent

Category	Old law	New law
Asset type		
Equipment	11	38
Structures	35	39
Inventory	58	48
Industry		
Agriculture	41	42
Mining	30	38
Oil extraction	23	28
Construction	28	41
Manufacturing	43	43
Transportation	23	37
Communications	24	36
Electric/gas	28	38
Trade	47	44
Services	32	40
Average	38	41

Source: Jane G. Gravelle, "Effective Corporate Tax Rates in the Major Tax Revision Plans: A Comparison of the House, Senate, and Conference Committtee Versions," Congressional Research Service Report 86-854 E, August 26, 1986, table 2.

rates on long-term capital gains would promote greater entrepreneurial daring.

While congressional intentions were well-meant, the capital gains exclusion was inefficient and produced serious side effects. The new rate structure weakens the case for retaining the exclusion. Furthermore, repeal of the exclusion will reduce incentives to invest in assets that have low pretax rates of return but lend themselves to converting ordinary income into capital gains. A standard ploy, for example, has been to borrow to buy an asset, then use deductions allowed for the interest paid on the borrowed money to offset fully taxable income, and ultimately sell the asset for a gain, 60 percent of which would be untaxed. Under prior law, a taxpayer in the 50 percent bracket who paid $100 in deductible interest and realized $100 in long-term capital gains would enjoy a gain of $30.[2]

Finally, the tax reform law simplifies the personal income tax for most taxpayers. Some of the 6 million taxpayers removed from the rolls because of lower rates will not even have to file. An additional 6 million taxpayers will no longer need to itemize deductions. Even more important than the simplification in filling

2. The taxpayer paid $100 in interest but saved $50 in taxes because the interest is deductible, for a net cost of $50. The tax liability would be only $20 on the $100 capital gain because only $40 of the gain would be subject to tax; hence the net gain is $80. The $80 net capital gain less the $50 net interest cost equals $30.

out one's return is the simplification that occurs because numerous provisions discourage tax-motivated investments and because the reduction of marginal tax rates curtails the importance of tax considerations on all transactions. Unfortunately, these gains in simplicity are offset to a considerable degree by new provisions that add to the complexity for a minority of taxpayers, as explained below.

What harm was done?

The most serious charge brought against the Tax Reform Act of 1986 is that it will increase the effective rate of tax on investment. There is something to this criticism, but much less than the average increase of corporate income taxes of $24 billion a year during 1987–91 would suggest (see table 6).

About half of this increase consists of tax changes that will not affect marginal investment decisions in most American industries. Other changes reduce deductions that do not enter into calculations of the profitability of a particular project—for example, limits on deductions for meals and entertainment. Still others increase taxes on investments abroad and may add to investment demand here—for example, some restrictions on the foreign tax credit. Another set of changes withdraws or reduces extreme advantages to

Table 6. *Estimated Revenue Increases in Corporate Income Tax, 1987–91*
Billions of dollars

Category	Amount
Specific items	**66.3**
Limitation on deductions for meals, travel, and entertainment	6.2
Repeal of sales tax deduction	1.3
Dividend-received deduction, other dividend changes, and change in liquidation rules	3.0
Compliance and tax administration	2.1
Financial institutions	8.3
Foreign tax provisions	9.3
Pensions and employee stock option plans	2.5
Insurance products and companies	11.5
Accounting provisions	21.5[a]
Intangible drilling and other mining costs except minimum tax	0.6
Other changes	**31.8**
Minimum tax	**22.2**
Overall increase	**120.3**

Source: *Tax Reform Act of 1986*, H. Rept. 99-841, vol. 2, 99 Cong. 2 sess. (Government Printing Office, 1986), table A.2, pp. II-866–84.
a. Includes $7.5 billion for repeal of reserves for bad debts of nonfinancial corporations; $9.6 billion on long-term contracts; $0.1 billion for qualified discount coupons; $1.5 billion for requiring utilities to accrue earned but unbilled income, and $2.8 billion for limits on use of cash accounting. Excludes $7.3 billion for recognition of gain on pledges of installment obligations; $32.2 billion for capitalization of inventory, construction, and development costs; $0.5 billion for contributions in aid of construction; and $0.3 billion for discharge of indebtedness.

particular industries—for example, taxes are increased on currently highly favored industries such as defense contractors, petroleum extraction, other mining, finance, and insurance. In addition, relatively few companies will be exposed to the minimum tax. These added tax liabilities will reduce corporate "cash flow" (the sum of after-tax earnings and depreciation reserves), a depressing influence on investment as a whole, but will not change most investment incentives at the margin.

For most companies, the increase in the effective rate of tax on investment will be small—from 38 percent to 41 percent, an 8 percent increase in effective rates.[3] This increase results from the repeal of the investment tax credit and amended depreciation deductions offset by lower corporate income tax rates. The 8 percent increase in *effective tax rates* contrasts with the 23 percent increase in *total collections* from all corporate taxpayers. The difference represents acceleration to 1987–91 of some tax payments that would not have been made until after 1991 under old law and some tax changes that affect cash flow.

However measured, the higher cost of capital to corporations will reduce incentives to invest. But this effect will be offset by the increased efficiency in the use of capital. Furthermore, monetary or fiscal policies that reduced interest rates by 0.8 percentage point would fully offset the increase in the cost of capital caused by revision of the corporate income tax.[4]

A second unfortunate characteristic of the reformed tax system is that it somewhat complicates the task of balancing the budget. Although the measure is revenue neutral over five years, it increases revenues in 1987 and decreases them in 1988 and 1989 (see table 7). Congress is using the 1987 windfall to avoid the nasty task of cutting spending or raising taxes to meet the fiscal 1987 deficit reduction targets of the Gramm-Rudman-Hollings act. Decreased revenues in the following two years, however, will make continued reduction of the federal deficit even more difficult than it has been so far.

Although the Tax Reform Act of 1986 may hinder deficit cuts in the short run, it could facilitate the eventual elimination of the budget deficit. By improving the fairness and reducing the distortions without sacrificing revenues, the tax reform act may

3. Jane G. Gravelle, "Effective Corporate Tax Rates in the Major Tax Revision Plans: A Comparison of the House, Senate, and Conference Committee Versions," Congressional Research Service Report 86-854 E, August 26, 1986, table 2.

4. Estimates reported to the author by Jane G. Gravelle, Congressional Research Service.

Table 7. *Estimated Effect of Tax Reform on Federal Revenues,*
Fiscal Years 1987–91
Billions of dollars

Fiscal year	Revenues
1987	11.4
1988	−16.7
1989	−15.1
1990	8.1
1991	12.0
1987–91	−0.3

Source: *Tax Reform Act of 1986,* H. Rept. 99-841, vol. 2, pp. II-884.

make it easier for Congress to raise taxes as part of a deficit reduction package.[5]

A final negative aspect of the new bill is that a minority of taxpayers will face a more complex tax system than they currently do. The expanded minimum tax is a set of provisions of labyrinthine obscurity. Various rules for recapturing at high incomes tax advantages permitted for low incomes add to the complexity for the small fraction of taxpayers to which they apply. These include the phaseout procedures that withdraw from high-income taxpayers the advantage of the 15 percent bracket, personal exemptions, deductions for contributions to individual retirement accounts, and deductions for up to $25,000 of losses on passive investments.

Much of this complexity results from the refusal of both the president and Congress to deal with fundamental inconsistencies that remain in the tax code. The phaseout rules permit Congress to maintain the fiction that the top marginal individual income tax rate is 28 percent. In fact, as noted earlier, it rises to 33 percent over the income range in which the phaseouts of the personal exemptions and 15 percent bracket occur.[6] And because Congress permitted some opportunities for tax avoidance to remain in the tax code, it was compelled to retain a minimum tax. The Treasury Department's proposal of November 1984 would have done away with the need for a minimum tax by eliminating directly the major devices for avoiding taxes.

What
opportunities
were missed?

The president and Congress missed three big opportunities for reform. First, they wasted an ideal chance to enact automatic adjustments to prevent inflation from distorting the measurement

5. James M. Buchanan, "Tax Reform and Political Choice," *Journal of Economic Perspectives,* forthcoming.

6. The tax law also contains other phaseouts—of the exclusion of contributions to individual retirement accounts, for example—that generate other effective marginal rates.

of capital income. Congress retained indexation of exemptions, the standard deduction, and tax brackets (first enacted in 1981), but did not adopt the Treasury Department proposal to index depreciation, interest payments and income, capital gains, and inventory costs. The absence of an automatic adjustment mechanism during the inflation of the late 1970s and early 1980s led Congress in 1978 to increase the proportion of long-term capital gains excluded from tax and in 1981 to enact a number of ad hoc provisions—notably depreciation deductions more favorable to some assets than to others—that contributed to the wide variations in effective tax rates among different types of assets. The Treasury Department's 1984 proposals would have removed the need for such adjustments during any future inflationary episode.

Unfortunately, the president rejected some of Treasury's recommendations, and Congress abandoned the rest. The fact that none was enacted demonstrates that indexation of the income tax base has little political sex appeal when inflation is low. However, if inflation reemerges, Congress will be pressured once again to enact ad hoc adjustments, which will leave a residue of distortion. The lesson that inflation can undermine a tax system has not yet been learned.

The president and Congress also failed to make any progress in two other areas that would have advanced equitable and efficient income taxation: the taxation of fringe benefits and the integration of the personal and corporate income taxes. The Tax Reform Act of 1986 does little to bring into the tax base fringe benefits that provide current consumption services to employees. Such fringes include employer-financed health insurance, up to $50,000 a year of term life insurance, group legal insurance, and assorted other items.

In 1982 President Reagan proposed limits on the exclusion from personal income tax of employer-purchased health insurance. He would have retained exclusion only up to a level sufficient to finance a fundamental health insurance plan; the cost of additional insurance was to be taxed as current income to employees. The Treasury Department incorporated this recommendation, along with other limits on the exclusion of fringe benefits, in its 1984 proposal. Faced with the unbending opposition of Senator Bob Packwood, chairman of the Senate Finance Committee, the president backed down and replaced the Treasury initiative with a watered-down proposal that had no appeal. The House Committee on Ways and Means killed the president's proposal and rejected all alternative devices for including consumption-type fringe benefits in taxable income.

While little was done to limit exclusion of fringe benefits, Congress enacted a variety of amendments to tighten existing rules designed to prevent such fringes from serving primarily high-income employees. These "nondiscrimination" rules typically require that no more than a stipulated fraction of a particular type of benefit can accrue to high-wage workers.

This outcome means that the tax system continues to favor certain kinds of consumption over others. Most notably, the tax system continues to encourage employees to seek and employers to provide excessively generous health insurance plans that promote medical cost inflation. It means that additional cuts in tax rates that would have been possible if fringe benefits had been included in the tax base had to be forgone. But it also means that such fringe benefits will be available more equally than in the past to low- and middle-wage workers.

The final missed opportunity was the failure to reduce the double taxation of dividend income. Under current law, dividend recipients are taxed twice—once indirectly by the corporate income tax, and once directly by the personal income tax. Most developed nations have instituted some relief for this double taxation.[7] The Treasury Department in 1984 proposed to permit corporations to deduct 50 percent of dividends paid. The White House scaled this deduction back to 10 percent, to be phased in over ten years. The House dropped the deduction altogether, and the Senate did not revive it.

The dividend deduction would have encouraged corporate managers to pay out a larger proportion of earnings in dividends. This incentive may explain its demise. If dividend payments increased, corporate managers would retain a smaller pool of earnings for new investment projects. They would have to rely to a greater extent than they now do on new issues of debt and equity to raise funds. Open market competition for investment funds might increase the efficiency with which those funds are allocated, but it would assuredly complicate the fund-raising tasks of corporate managers. The current tax policy of discouraging payment of dividends lessens this particular managerial headache. The lack of enthusiasm among corporate managers for a dividend deduction, which made it easy for the White House and Congress to jettison the proposal, probably owes something to this fact of corporate financial life.

7. Joseph A. Pechman, "Tax Reform Prospects in Europe and Canada," *Brookings Review,* vol. 5 (Winter 1987), pp. 11–19.

What will be the economic effects?

The effects of the tax bill on overall economic performance are likely to be small. The shift in taxes from individuals to corporations will cause an increase in personal disposable income. Because consumption is closely tied to personal disposable income, consumption outlays may go up in 1987 and beyond. Because deductions for state and local sales taxes will be repealed as of January 1, 1987, the bill may also cause some increase in purchases of costly consumer durable goods during the last quarter of 1986.

The overall effects on investment are difficult to gauge because many offsetting factors are at work. On one hand, the increase in corporate income taxes will reduce corporate cash flow, a development that, as noted, will discourage corporate investment. The increase in the effective tax rate on investment will also tend to reduce investment.

On the other hand, the same increase in effective tax rates will increase the tendency for the value of the U.S. dollar to fall, a development that should make U.S. goods more competitive in international markets. This effect follows because higher taxes will reduce the appeal of U.S. assets relative to foreign assets and thereby reduce the demand for U.S. dollars. Additional decline in the value of the dollar will improve U.S. competitiveness. Whether the dollar's decline will also increase investment depends on what happens to U.S. interest rates.

While the tax reform will have only modest effects on the economy as a whole, it will have important effects on particular industries and companies. For example, the cost of capital for such tax shelter investments as office buildings and multifamily housing will increase. Other industries, such as trade, computers, and some manufacturing, will gain more from lower tax rates and liberalized depreciation on equipment than they will lose from repeal of the investment tax credit and slower depreciation on structures.

Eliminating tax preferences that hampered investment efficiency and the growth of economic capacity was a primary objective of tax reform. But there is no way to correct past imbalances and achieve these gains in efficiency without shifting tax burdens among industries. And when tax incentives that have contributed to overinvestment in favored activities are reduced, the adjustments may be difficult and protracted. For example, the vacancy rates for offices, which exceed 20 percent in many cities and are attributable in part to tax shelters that encouraged construction even when potential occupants could not be identified, will take many years to decline to economically efficient levels.

A final
appraisal

Although these missed opportunities and the harmful elements of the tax reform should not be ignored—if possible, they should be corrected in future legislation—they should not obscure the major achievements in the Tax Reform Act of 1986. By removing millions of poor families from the tax rolls and reducing the burdens of millions of other low-income families, by slashing marginal tax rates and thereby reducing the importance of taxes in economic decisions, by ending the distinction between long-term and short-term capital gains and thereby reducing the incentives to engage in complex tax-avoidance maneuvers, by curbing tax shelters, and by equalizing effective tax rates on various kinds of investment, the tax bill represents a significant improvement in the structure of personal and corporate income taxes. That a good bill contains flaws, some of them important, may make us yearn for what might have been, but it should not prevent us from celebrating a splendid political and economic achievement.

Comments by Thomas S. Neubig

IN DISCUSSIONS of tax reform, most analysts fit into one of four categories. First, there are those who are happy only if the glass is entirely full. They wistfully speak of Treasury I and how far the final bill was from that earlier proposal. But these supporters of a pure income tax generally gloss over the long list of politically determined provisions that were kept out of that document. For those who want to know, most of them are listed on page 7 of Treasury I, including mortgage interest deductions, state and local tax-exempt bonds, and tax-exempt social security benefits.

The second group of analysts are unhappy because this tax reform was not at all their cup of tea. The reform swung the pendulum back toward an income tax, and the crowd favoring a consumption tax stood on the sidelines. Most of them do not favor a true progressive consumption tax but prefer a regressive value-added tax or a bastardized version of a consumption tax that does not apply to investments while continuing to allow a deduction for interest. We will hear more from this group as they try to swing the pendulum back in their direction.

The third group always sees the glass as half empty. There were some improvements, they admit, but they are more interested in discussing the problems with tax reform. Most analysts working "inside the Beltway" fall into this category, always limiting their discussions to what their clients should worry about next. For instance, the concern about the top marginal tax rate being 33 percent rather than 28 percent is legitimate, but does it merit all the attention it has received, when it affects less than 5 percent of all taxpayers? The same concern has not been expressed about the phaseout of the graduated corporate tax rates with a 51 percent marginal tax rate under prior law.

Henry Aaron does not fit into any of these three groups. His paper lists the accomplishments of the Tax Reform Act of 1986 while making a realistic assessment of some of its drawbacks and the opportunities missed. He sees the glass as at least half full, possibly three-quarters full, rather than half empty. I include myself in this fourth group not only because I have spent two and one-half years of my life working on this bill, but because I consider the tax reform process as incremental. I agree with most of the accomplishments, concerns, and missed opportunities that Aaron identifies, but would like to comment on four issues he raised.

First, Aaron cites lower marginal tax rates as a major accomplishment of the 1986 act, but then discusses only the relatively small expected effect on labor supply. Lower marginal tax rates have a number of other potential benefits, however, and although some of them have been oversold, let me mention two important ones.

The tax reform act is lauded for repealing and changing many tax preferences, thus reducing the influence of government on everyday economic decisions. The Joint Committee on Taxation and the Treasury Department measure these tax preferences annually in the tax expenditure budget. Although provisions to repeal and scale back items will reduce the tax expenditure budget, the reduction in marginal tax rates will have an even bigger effect simply by reducing the value of all remaining tax benefits.

Many analysts have bemoaned the fact that tax reform left intact the mortgage interest deduction on owner-occupied homes. They do not mention that lower marginal tax rates have reduced the value of mortgage interest deductions significantly. For top-bracket individuals the value is reduced by 44 percent (from fifty cents on the dollar to only twenty-eight cents). The same reduced value applies to fringe benefits, the investment income earned in life insurance policies, and many other tax benefits.

Lawrence Lindsey of Harvard University has found that the biggest potential effect on taxable income of lower marginal tax rates is not the possible response of labor supply but rather the response by taxpayers switching from tax-preferred activities to fully taxable activities, such as reductions in business entertainment expenses and itemized deductions.[8] Changing investment portfolios and consumption decisions may greatly increase future revenues, but that effect generally was not included in the bill's revenue estimates.[9]

Second, Aaron applauds the increased efficiency in capital investment due to the reduced variation in effective tax rates among assets and industries, yet he worries about the impact of higher effective tax rates on those same investments. One of the interesting developments during the legislative process was the discussion among economists about the effect on the quantity of investment versus the effect on the efficiency or quality of investment. This trade-off between quantity and quality is an empirical one, but the large-scale macromodels forecast changes in only the quantity of investment and generally do not incorporate improved efficiency of the capital stock. Recent work by Don Fullerton and James Mackie with a general equilibrium model indicates that improvement in the efficiency of the capital stock from tax reform more than offsets any decline in quantity.[10] Clearly, less can be better if it is more efficient.

Third, Aaron cites as missed opportunities the failure to enact automatic adjustments for inflation, taxation of fringe benefits, and integration of the personal and corporate income taxes. I would agree and add two more. First, tax reform failed to systematically address general savings and retirement incentives in the tax code. Where in the hybrid income–consumption tax world the tax system should be was not addressed directly. Thus IRAs, 401s, Keoghs, pension plans, life insurance policies, housing, and tax-exempt bonds were all considered separately, instead of as a unified whole. One could argue that Congress did consider each of these and thus did make an explicit decision. However, I do not believe that the issue was ever framed in a systematic way, not even in Treasury I.

The second missed opportunity occurred because of the focus on revenue estimates for five years only. For example, taxation of the inside buildup on life insurance policies was taken off the

8. Lawrence B. Lindsey, "Individual Taxpayer Response to Tax Cuts 1982–1984 with Implications for the Revenue-Maximizing Tax Rate," National Bureau of Economic Research Working Paper 2069 (Cambridge, Mass.: NBER, November 1986).

9. For a discussion of some of the behavioral effects incorporated into Treasury revenue estimates, see Howard Nester, "Revenue Estimates: Macro Static/Micro Dynamic," *National Tax Association–Tax Institute of America Annual Conference Proceedings—1986*, forthcoming.

10. Don Fullerton, Yolanda K. Henderson, and James Mackie, "Investment Allocation and Growth under the Tax Reform Act of 1986," U.S. Department of the Treasury, Office of Tax Analysis, December 1986.

table not because it was a bad idea but because it raised no significant revenue during the first five years, when all existing policies were grandfathered. Revenue estimates limited to five years biased reform toward short-term revenue raisers while ignoring future revenue losses.

Finally, a comment on the issue of simplicity. Too often simplicity is measured by the number of pages in the Internal Revenue Code, or the length of the tax forms, or even the number of tax brackets. In fact, the number of tax brackets has no significance for most taxpayers, who use tax schedules with tax liability already calculated for them. Aaron is correct that fewer people will file returns, more taxpayers will file shorter returns, and fewer taxpayers will itemize deductions. But most important, the bill will simplify the lives of all taxpayers by reducing tax considerations in everyday investment and consumption decisions.

From the outset, efficiency, equity, and simplicity were seen as desirable goals, but it was recognized that an efficient and fair income tax system requires accurate measurement of economic income that is often complex. The well-to-do who are affected by the minimum tax, the limitations on passive losses, and the tax on minors' unearned income will find the tax system more complicated, though some of them make it complicated for themselves by attempting to use every possible tax preference in the code. Businesses will also find the system more complicated because of tougher cost capitalization rules, an alternative minimum tax, and four depreciation systems—one for the regular tax, one for the minimum tax, one for the book-income preference item, and one for the calculation of earnings and profits. Clearly, some provisions can be further rationalized and simplified.

Aaron's paper is an insightful and useful summary of the tax reform act. He has surely heard the advantages of lower marginal tax rates lauded more than I, so it is natural for him to concentrate on the effects of other provisions. However, in terms of efficiency, equity, and simplicity, the many benefits of lower marginal tax rates should not be overlooked.

The Tax Reform Act of 1986 was not a revolution, but with its broader tax base and lower marginal tax rates it turned out to be not an impossible dream.

Comments by Randall D. Weiss

HENRY AARON has done a fine job of describing the highlights of the 1986 tax reform act. I certainly agree that by the traditional standards of tax policy—equity, efficiency, and simplicity—this act represents a significant improvement in the income tax. I would like to emphasize the horizontal equity aspects of the legislation and to question the assertion that indexing and integration should have been incorporated into the tax code at this time.

One of the principal themes of the act, and certainly the principal political force behind it, was to improve the fairness of the income tax. Aaron presents the data documenting the increase in progressivity achieved by this legislation, a deliberate choice of Congress. Even more important, in my view, was the improvement in horizontal equity. Under the old system, many individuals with substantial incomes and corporations that reported large profits to their shareholders paid little or no income tax. This was the most visible characteristic of a system that performed poorly under the traditional notion that taxpayers with equal ability to pay should have the same tax liability. Among members of Congress, a perception had developed that the American public thought that the tax system was very unfair. The relatively few members who ultimately opposed tax reform did not defend the present system. Rather, they argued that they would have supported a better version of tax reform. The act's systematic attack on horizontal inequity, in view of the public perception of unfairness, was the main feature that led to its enactment.

The proliferation of tax shelters was perhaps the most apparent feature of a system in which the tax base did not correlate well with economic income, and Aaron rightly mentions the attack on tax shelters as one of the most significant features of the act. It should be emphasized, however, that tax shelters are merely one very visible means of transferring tax benefits from those individuals who cannot use them to those who can. For example, someone who wants to build a building may find, especially if the building is highly leveraged, that he would have large tax benefits that he could not use immediately or perhaps could never use. Rather than allow the value of these benefits to decrease, such a person would market the losses, typically through limited partnerships, to others for whom the losses are of immediate benefit. The large expansion of this sort of activity led to a situation in which many individuals with high economic incomes were paying little or no tax. The passive loss provisions of the act were a direct response to this phenomenon.

Many of the other provisions of the act involved modifications of tax benefits that often were transferred in ordinary business transactions. It is interesting that a search for provisions in prior

law that led to the perception of unfairness resulted in many
limitations on benefits that often were transferred, as well as direct
limitations on the transfers. For example, the investment credit
and depreciation benefits were often transferred through leasing
and tax shelter activity. Much of the use of debt finance, as Gene
Steuerle has pointed out in his discussion of tax arbitrage, is an
attempt to transfer the benefit of low tax rates to taxpayers with
higher rates. The dividend-received deduction generates a tax
benefit for corporate purchasers of stock that often is issued by
corporations that could not have used interest deductions if debt,
rather than equity, had been the financing vehicle. The transfer
of net operating losses from a selling corporation to an acquiring
one involves direct transfer of tax benefits. The act limited the
deductions available for property and casualty insurance reserves;
such operations had so consistently generated tax losses that they
were being acquired by corporations that could make current use
of the losses. The prior law's rules for installment sales and
corporate liquidations encouraged the transfer of used assets that
were not generating deductions in the hands of one taxpayer to
another taxpayer who could use deductions, and these were
tightened considerably. The low tax rates associated with treating
children as separate taxpayers were a tax benefit available to
parents who transferred assets into the child's name; this too was
restricted by the act. Finally, the issuance of tax-exempt bonds,
which represent a transfer of the benefit of tax exemption from
state and local governments to high-income individuals, was
severely restricted under the act.

It would be an exaggeration to argue that Congress's explicit
goal in the 1986 act was to attack tax benefits that could not be
fully used by their intended beneficiary. It appears, however, that
an attempt to restore a perception of fairness to the tax system
led naturally to these restrictions.

As an aside, it should be noted many of these tax provisions
may have had less actual incentive effect than typical illustrative
calculations have indicated. For example, many of the users of
capital received the benefit of the investment credit and rapid
depreciation not as a reduction in their own taxes, but rather as
a reduction in rents paid to a leasing intermediary. Because of
numerous transactions costs and inefficiencies in the market for
tax benefits, lessees have received less incentive from these
provisions than direct users of the tax benefits. Thus withdrawal
of these benefits from the economy, averaging over both owner-
users and lessees, will actually have less of an effect than indicated

by illustrations that assume direct use. The assumption of direct use is usually built into calculations of the so-called effective tax rate or cost of capital. A paradigm of the inefficiency of transferred tax benefits, of course, is the tax exemption of state and local bonds; economists have long argued that the high–income individuals who are the intermediaries in these transactions receive a significant portion of the tax benefits.

Let me now turn to two of the subjects that Aaron asserted were missed opportunities—indexing and integration. Putting politics aside, I believe that there were good substantive reasons not to enact either last year.

The biggest question about indexing the definition of capital income is whether it is feasible. The problem posed by indexing within the current economic environment is that financial transactions in the U.S. economy are not indexed as a general rule, unlike the situation in many of the countries that have implemented indexing. Thus indexing would involve imposing new concepts and definitions of financial and real transactions that are not reflected in the terms of the transactions themselves. The most difficult part of indexing, in my view, is dividing interest income and deductions into real and inflationary components. Treasury I contained the most recent proposal to do this. Unfortunately, this proposal deviated significantly from economic reality by assuming that the inflationary component of all interest payments made within a period was a fixed proportion that was uniform across all debt. Thus the proposal ignored the differences in real interest rates that result from differences in risk and maturity among different debt instruments. It is not clear that, on the average, this proposal would have improved the measurement of economic income and thus achieved the goal of reducing the variance in the rate of taxation of capital income across taxpayers and time periods. (A similar question can be raised with respect to capital gains; it is not clear whether, on the average, indexed realized gain performs better than unindexed realized gain when measured against the ideal of indexed *accrued* gain.)

If a feasible proposal has not been developed to index interest income and deductions, then there is a serious question about whether it is appropriate to index only some aspects of the definition of capital income. Certainly such action would not move the tax system closer to indexing proponents' avowed goal of better measurement of the real income of each taxpayer. The sensitivity of capital costs in different sectors could still be quite large. Further, indexing of depreciation deductions without indexing debt, for example, could result during inflationary periods in a huge increase in tax deductions among taxpayers with leveraged investments and could exacerbate the tax arbitrage problem discussed above.

The last points to consider about indexing are those which caused the most concern among the members of Congress. Indexing may substantially increase the sensitivity of the government's revenues to inflation, risking an unwanted increase in the deficit. Finally, conceptually sound proposals to index interest and capital gain would involve enormous complexity. For all these reasons, especially given the low rates of inflation expected in the near future, I do not think enactment of indexing provisions in last year's act would have been prudent.

As for corporate integration, certainly Aaron is correct that corporate managers would not like to have increased pressure to pay dividends, which restricts political support for integration proposals. But I also believe that this lack of support reflects some lack of understanding within the economics profession of what the effects of integration would be. The double taxation of dividends is really voluntary. Corporations do not have to pay out dividends, and some pay none or have a very low payout rate. Double taxation of dividends is reduced to the extent dividends are reduced, of course, and the only other double taxation of corporate earnings that might occur would be the capital gains tax on the disposition of stock. This tax is typically deferred or avoided entirely. Given this situation, it is difficult to know why corporations pay dividends and thus what the economic effects of dividend relief might be.

It should also be noted that many of the alleged effects of double taxation were addressed by other aspects of the act. The bias toward debt finance was dealt with by reducing the corporate tax rate and tightening the rules affecting the benefit of interest deductions for multinational corporations. The effect on the cost of corporate capital was addressed through the rate and the depreciation system. Double taxation was also accused of encouraging corporate distributions in the form of takeovers, but that has been discouraged by the repeal of the exemption for corporate capital gain realized on liquidation and by the taxation of individual capital gain at the same rate as ordinary income. Thus, given the present state of knowledge about the effects of double taxation, it is not clear to me that it would improve economic efficiency to increase the corporate tax rate or scale back the acceleration of depreciation to pay for a provision granting dividend relief.

In sum, Aaron has done an excellent job at summing up the accomplishments of the 1986 tax reform act, but I believe that considerably more technical and economic exploration is required before indexing and integration should be seriously considered for enactment.

Effects on Industry

LARRY L. DILDINE

BY THE TIME the Tax Reform Act of 1986 was signed, the newspapers and news magazines had generally characterized the new law as a landmark of tax legislation. The conventional synopsis of the new law predicted the following major consequences: lower taxes for most individual taxpayers, no taxes for the working poor, higher taxes for those with tax shelters, higher taxes for business, loss of saving and investment incentives, "revenue neutrality," and a shift of $120 billion in tax from individuals to business.

Economic forecasters and commentators reached similar if somewhat more detailed conclusions. They generally agreed that the new law would be hard on real estate and capital formation but good for consumers and labor-intensive businesses. Some expected a temporary stimulus, followed by an investment slump. Some also saw long-term efficiency gains from more productive uses of available capital.

A closer look at the consequences of tax reform, especially as applied to business, will confirm much of what has been written in the press. But it will also reveal some misleading oversimplifications. In particular, it is worthwhile to consider carefully some of the details behind the well-publicized five-year revenue estimates.

Analyzing the revenue estimates

The Joint Committee on Taxation estimates that corporations will pay an additional tax of $120.3 billion in 1987–91. At the same time, individuals will receive a net reduction of $120.5 billion in income and excise taxes. Overall, the joint committee certified the new law to be revenue neutral.

The summary estimates of corporate and individual revenues are often discussed as if they indicate a general increase in business taxes and a tax cut for households. But a closer look at these

The author wishes to thank Robert Patrick, Kenneth Wertz, and Eugene Steuerle for helpful suggestions.

31

numbers reveals a smaller *general* corporate tax increase; most of the higher taxes are concentrated on particular industries and certain transactions. Conversely, the tax reduction for individuals masks some very significant tax increases imposed on unincorporated business activities and individual business interests. Also, some of the business tax increases are "speedups" of deferred tax liabilities, rather than permanent increases.

Only a few provisions of the new law can be regarded as imposing general business tax increases. These include the repeal of the investment tax credit, changes in depreciation allowances, cutback of the dividend deduction, uniform capitalization rules for inventories, and limitations on deductions for meals, travel, and entertainment. Offsetting these to some extent are the corporate rate reductions and the extension of the tax credit for research and experimentation, which is widely claimed by corporations. The other corporate tax increases (and a few reductions) apply predominantly to specific industries or particular types of transactions. These industry-specific changes account for about 60 percent of the total corporate tax increase. Revenue estimates for these general and specific corporate provisions are given in table 1.

However one measures the revenue effects on corporations, it is important to keep in mind that the estimates are for five years, not one, and they represent only corporations, not all business. On an annual basis, the increase in corporate tax is not so large: $24 billion a year is about 8 percent of net corporate income and 5 percent of annual spending for business plant and equipment. Tax changes of such magnitude may be very important in any particular industry, but dire predictions or extravagant hopes about the entire economy are unwarranted, at least in the short run.

Politicians and pundits tend to forget that corporations cannot really pay taxes; taxes must ultimately be borne by the real people who are the corporation's owners, managers, employees, customers, and suppliers. Most public finance specialists agree that corporate tax increases are borne mainly by suppliers of capital. The importance of a general corporate tax increase is its effect on the amount of capital supplied to corporate enterprises. The importance of specific tax increases is their effect on the directing of capital among alternative uses, both corporate and noncorporate.

There is a corollary to the adage that corporations don't pay taxes, people pay taxes. The corollary (which corporate spokesmen tend to forget) is that the individual tax applies to business, too.

Table 1. *Estimated Revenues from Corporate Tax Provisions in the Tax Reform Act of 1986, 1987–91*
Billions of dollars

Corporate provision	Revenue
General	
Investment tax credit	118.7
Depreciation, expensing	7.7
Dividends received	1.1
Inventory capitalization	32.2
Rate reductions	−116.7
Research credits	−3.9
Limits on business meals	6.2
Total	45.4
Specific	
Rehabilitation tax credit	0.9
Natural resources	0.6
General utilities	1.7
Long-term contracts	9.6
Recognition of gain on installment sales	7.3
Small business last in, first out accounting	−1.8
Contributions in aid of construction	0.5
Financial institutions	8.3
Insurance products and companies	11.5
Pensions and deferred compensation	2.5
Foreign tax provisions	9.3
Alternative minimum tax	22.2
Total	72.6
Other (including tax-exempt bonds, compliance and tax administration, and miscellaneous corporate provisions)	2.3
Total	120.3

Source: *Tax Reform Act of 1986*, H. Rept. 99-841, vol. 2, 99 Cong. 2 sess. (Government Printing Office, 1986), pp. II-865–85.

Individual rate reductions apply to business income, and most base-broadening provisions apply to individuals as well as corporations. A full accounting for changes in business taxation requires adding certain individual tax items to the corporate estimates.

The tax changes that apply to business income taxed to individuals are summarized in table 2. Leaving aside the offsetting effect of rate reductions, these provisions add up to an additional tax increase for business of $90 billion. Like the tax increases for corporations, these are mainly concentrated in particular sectors and activities.

Base broadening for noncorporate business will be offset to some degree by individual rate reductions. It is difficult to separate out the effect of rate reduction on business income alone. But the net business income of taxpayers who reported net income from

Table 2. *Estimated Revenues from Business Tax Provisions*
Applying to Individuals, 1987–91
Billions of dollars

Provision	Revenue
Depreciation	4.7
Business meals	5.3
Investment tax credit	24.2
Rehabilitation tax credit	3.0
Low-income housing credit	−3.2
At-risk rules	1.8
Passive loss limitation	36.0
Individual alternative minimum tax	8.2
Dividend exclusion	2.6
Regulated investment companies	1.9
Inventory capitalization	2.5
Partnership, subchapter S, and personal service tax year conformity	1.7
Tax-exempt bonds	0.7
Resources	1.0
Total	90.3

Source: *Tax Reform Act of 1986*, H. Rept. 99-841, vol. 2, pp. II-865–85.

businesses of all kinds accounted for about 10 percent of total adjusted gross income in a recent year. If as much as 20 percent of the rate cuts are allocable to this income, the rate reduction would be worth only $41 billion, leaving a net additional tax on business of nearly $50 billion at the individual level.[1]

Revenue estimates fall far short of telling the whole quantitative story of the new law. Some of the estimates reflect permanent tax changes, such as rate reductions and repeal of the investment tax credit, while others are mainly one-time speedups of tax collections. A number of the largest five-year totals are for items that decrease after a year or two. These include the individual and corporate minimum taxes and all of the changes in accounting rules. Indeed, the revenue increases from accounting rule changes were deliberately timed to cover the five-year budget period, after which they produce relatively little revenue.

For some past tax bills, the Treasury Department estimated the annual revenue effect of each provision after all transitional effects were completed. Such long-run, full-effect estimates would give a more accurate picture of the importance of the provisions for economic incentives and would also indicate whether future tax bills might be required to maintain revenue neutrality. Clearly,

1. Individual rate reductions are estimated to save taxpayers $207.1 billion, of which 20 percent would be $41.4 billion. Thus $90.3 billion of base broadening is offset by about $41.4 billion of rate reductions, leaving $48.9 billion of net tax increase.

the accounting rule changes and the minimum taxes would emerge as less important in the long run than they are over the five-year projection period.

If the new law is to remain revenue neutral, the revenue from some other provisions must grow disproportionately over time. The changes in depreciation fulfill this purpose during the five-year accounting period. While the combined revenue from accounting rules and minimum taxes falls from $25.2 billion in 1988 to $14.6 billion in 1991, the revenue effect of changing depreciation allowances increases from −$3.4 billion to $12.5 billion. The increase due to depreciation will also be largely temporary, however. The increase arises because depreciation deductions are speeded up for short-lived property and slowed down for longer-lived assets. Thus the negative effects occur mainly in the first few years, then the increased revenues prevail, and finally, as most assets come under the new system, the increased revenues will settle down to a smaller but growing level as capital spending continues to grow. The peak year for added revenues due to depreciation is probably about 1991. Thus the new law probably has a built-in tendency to lose revenue over time.

One other fact of life will reinforce the tendency toward revenue shortfall: most behavioral changes will be in the direction of tax avoidance. In fairness, many of the first-order behaviors are already built into the estimates. For example, the estimators have allowed a loss of $12.6 billion for the anticipated shift of real estate and other tax shelter activity to the corporate sector. Another decrease of $3.3 billion is estimated to result from the shift of tax-exempt bonds from financial institutions to households. Such shifts are accounted for whenever they are at all predictable. But a massive change in the tax law will undoubtedly induce large second- and third-order changes in the economy. These movements will include shifts of business among industries, a general realignment of balance sheets, and in particular a greater use of "passthrough" entities to avoid the much-expanded corporate tax.

The current state of the art in economics simply does not allow for quantitative estimation of these large-scale microeconomic changes over a five-year period. The only certainty is that the direction of the changes is toward reduced revenues, because saving taxes is the principal motivation for such behavior.

Despite the above reservations, I conclude that the new law comes sufficiently close to the intended revenue neutrality that analysis should concentrate on predicting shifts of economic activity among markets, sectors, and business practices rather than the unpredictable short-term macroeconomic concerns of employment and GNP growth. I will now attempt to assess some of these sectoral shifts.

The great asset swap

One of the key features of the tax reform act is a fundamental change in the relative tax treatment of corporations compared with that of individual investors. Rather than moving in the direction of integrating the corporate and individual taxes, as most tax reform proposals have suggested and many other countries have done, the new law has moved in a way that can fairly be described as disintegration. The corporate double tax has been strengthened and some business activities may be forced toward the corporate sector. Three provisions account for most of this change and others reinforce them.

First, the maximum rate has been reduced more for individuals than for corporations. Thus in many instances the marginal tax rate applicable to the corporation will be substantially higher than the rate for major shareholders as individuals. Second, increased share values resulting from reinvestment of after-tax corporate earnings will now result in full taxation of individuals' capital gains. Third, activities that have been conducted in noncorporate form, such as real estate and minerals development, may now be more attractive for corporations because any losses created may be usable by corporations but denied to individuals under the passive loss rules.

Two other changes are further evidence of the move to disintegrate the corporate tax. The new law reverses a long-standing rule—known as "General Utilities"—that has allowed appreciated property in corporations to escape the corporate tax in certain liquidations. Also, the new law increases from 15 to 20 percent the amount of a corporate dividend that will be taxed to an unrelated corporation that receives it. Such distributions are from income that has already been subject to corporate tax at least once. While this form of corporate double tax has often been justified on the grounds that much corporate income escapes tax the first time, it is difficult to see the justification for raising the percentage of double tax on dividends at the same time the corporate tax base is being broadened.

The practical effect of relative changes in corporate and individual taxation is to encourage trading of ownership of business assets between the sectors to achieve better "matchups." Real estate, equipment leasing, and other tax shelter activities can be expected to move to corporations and other institutional ownership. Businesses that grow from plowing back profits will get much better tax treatment if organized as partnerships or structured as corporations that are taxed as partnerships.

Asset swaps will add to business in the first year or two for those who earn commissions or otherwise facilitate deals. More significant for the longer term, however, the new tax law will cause substantial changes in the relative cost of various products and services. It will also alter product demands. These sectoral microeconomic effects are the real business story of the new tax law.

Effects on individual sectors

A major objective of the tax reform legislation was to broaden the corporate tax base, so that each dollar of corporate earnings would attract more nearly the same tax. Combined with rate reduction, the broadening of the tax base will increase costs for some types of business while reducing them for others.

Equipment-Intensive Manufacturing

Without question, industries that regularly invest a large share of their earnings in machinery and equipment will encounter higher costs under the new tax law. It is too general to say that this is true of all capital-intensive business because inventories, buildings, intangibles, and receivables are capital, too; but equipment costs are clearly raised by the repeal of the investment tax credit. This repeal is the source of the largest single tax increase in the new law. New depreciation rules also raise the cost of many types of equipment, especially those with longer lives. These include most industrial machinery, although the change from five years at roughly 150 percent declining balance to seven years at 200 percent declining balance is not large.

One summary measure of the tax effect on equipment costs is to consider the pretax rate of return required to attain a target after-tax yield. Unlike revenue estimates, this measure properly focuses the attention on the amount of income left after taxes—the real economic motivation—not on the amount of tax payment.

Consider an item of industrial machinery classified as ten-year property under the pre-1981 asset depreciation range (ADR) system. Under old law the up-front benefits of the investment tax credit and accelerated depreciation are worth slightly more than the future taxes due as taxable income is eventually earned. Thus a pretax return of 7.6 percent is sufficient to yield 8.0 percent after tax.[2] Under new law, including the substantial corporate

2. These rates include an assumed inflation rate of 4 percent. It is also assumed that all deductions and credits are currently usable to the acquiring company.

rate reduction, a pretax yield of 9.5 percent would be required from the same type of property to achieve 8.0 percent after corporate tax—a 25 percent increase in the required return.

Other provisions of importance to equipment-intensive businesses are more difficult to quantify. Perhaps the most significant is the new alternative minimum tax for corporations. This provision applies a rate of 20 percent to a broader measure of taxable income that includes slower depreciation (generally 150 percent declining balance over the old guideline period) and half of any additional amount of reported book profit. This untaxed book profit will commonly be due to slower depreciation as well. After limited allowances for prior-year losses, foreign tax credits, and remaining investment tax credit carryovers, if the 20 percent minimum tax exceeds the regular 34 percent tax in any year, the corporation must pay the higher tax. In subsequent years, the cumulative amount of additional minimum tax will be paid back to the extent that regular tax would be higher in those years. Thus, except in rare cases where large deferrals of regular tax persist, the alternative minimum tax is at most a prepayment of regular tax. Even when the tax is not owed, it is a considerable nuisance to corporate accounting and investment planning.

A persistent minimum tax due to accelerated depreciation will be rare for any corporation because year-by-year depreciation allowances tend to equalize any two systems of depreciation once they have been in place for one replacement cycle. What remains of the difference is due to growth or cyclical factors. For a minimum tax to persist, additional preference items must equal at least 70 percent of regular taxable income every year.[3]

Very few companies will have sustained growth sufficient to continue producing depreciation deferral equal to 70 percent of regular taxable income, unless they have chronically low profit rates or large loss carryovers. During the first replacement cycle following the introduction of the minimum tax, however, slower depreciation for new assets will cause minimum taxable income to diverge substantially from regular income, especially in cases (such as steel products manufacturing) where depreciation periods are much longer for the minimum tax than for regular tax. The minimum tax is, therefore, largely a transition provision that will add to the cost of equipment for the first replacement cycle. It will apply selectively thereafter, especially in periods of depressed

3. For example, if the regular tax is $34 on $100 of taxable income, the minimum tax will apply only if "alternative minimum taxable income," taxed at 20 percent, is more than $170.

profitability or high growth or in years following net operating losses.

Manufacturing companies of all kinds will also suffer some adverse short-term effects from the changes in accounting rules, particularly those changes that apply to inventories and installment sales. Under the new inventory accounting rules, a number of new items must be capitalized into the cost of inventory rather than currently expensed. These include accelerated depreciation, current pension and fringe benefit costs, and a portion of general and administrative costs. The installment-sale rules call for current recognition of income on installment sales in proportion to the ratio of debt to total assets on the company's balance sheet. This proportionate disallowance rule introduces to the tax code the highly dubious proposition that borrowing may sometimes represent income. This rule is apparently a crude proxy for recognizing an installment sale as a sale combined with a loan to the buyer with imputed interest. These accounting changes mainly represent one-time speedups in recognition of income (spread over a statutory four-year period); they will have an adverse effect on cash flows but a relatively small effect on the prospective cost of capital.

Higher costs do not always imply that a particular economic sector will shrink relative to others. The new tax law will also influence the demand in each industrial sector. Tax reductions for middle- and upper-income households will probably stimulate spending for consumer durables. Generally lower interest rates caused by lower taxes on savers may also contribute to demand for durables, despite the offsetting loss of deductions for interest on consumer loans. A full analysis of the tax impact in any sector requires an evaluation of the demand effects as well as the changes in business costs.

Mature Manufacturing

Despite the large increase in corporate tax collections, some types of manufacturing will have lower tax costs. Certain mature industries, for example, require relatively little annual investment in capital equipment to maintain productive capacity and avoid obsolescence. Those with stable markets and consistent profit rates—for example, the food, beverage, and apparel industries— paid high effective tax rates under old law. Companies specializing in these sectors will normally benefit more from corporate rate reduction than they lose in investment tax credits, depreciation, and accounting changes. The alternative minimum tax is also less likely to be a problem, except for those with loss carryovers that would have wiped out regular tax. On the demand side, because these businesses are often consumer oriented their markets may increase due to individual tax reduction.

High-Tech Manufacturing

The high-tech industries are those with large annual spending for research and high average rates of profit, reflecting a premium for high risk. Their assets are predominantly intangibles and short-lived equipment. Domestic businesses in these industries are likely to benefit from the new law as rate reductions bring down historically high corporate tax rates. Exceptions are high-tech companies that produce and sell under long-term contracts.

Research expenses will continue to be deductible and the incremental research credit will still be available (at a rate that is now larger relative to the tax rate), but with tighter rules for eligibility. Demand for the products of these industries—computers, medical equipment, electronics, aerospace, defense equipment, and scientific instruments—will be aided or not greatly harmed by the new law.

Multinationals

Many detailed technical changes have been made in the taxation of multinational companies. None will have a greater effect, however, than simple rate reduction.

U.S.-based companies with operations in high-tax countries (for example, most of Europe and Japan) will be much more likely to encounter a limitation on the amount of their foreign taxes that can be credited against the U.S. tax. The new law will reduce the rate of U.S. tax without expanding the amount of taxable foreign-source income. (The investment tax credit and accelerated depreciation were not previously allowed for foreign operations.) Since the amount of credit for foreign taxes is generally limited to the U.S. rate on foreign-source income, excess credits would become more common due to rate reduction alone. The tendency toward excess credits is reinforced by new source rules that allocate more interest and other fungible costs to offset foreign-source income and by new foreign tax credit limitation rules that require the limitation calculation to be made separately for different "baskets" of income. These new rules will especially limit the foreign tax credit in the case of U.S. companies with affiliated foreign banking operations.

A U.S. company with excess foreign tax credits may now seek to locate or expand operations in a low-tax country in order to reduce its average foreign tax rate, although such suitable locations are limited. Those with operations in both high- and low-tax countries may also find that no additional tax will result from repatriation of earnings from low-tax countries, so that they may be encouraged to reinvest foreign earnings in the United States. The expansion in the new law of Subpart F rules (terminating tax deferral for undistributed earnings of certain foreign corporations) will also have the effect of encouraging repatriation.

Foreign-based multinationals with U.S. manufacturing operations will generally encounter higher taxes in the United States, just as domestic companies do. The extent to which these taxes are offset at home varies widely among countries. Except where the additional tax is fully credited, the tendency toward higher U.S. taxes will work against foreign investment in the United States.

The short-run consequences for U.S. trade will probably depend on the relative strengths of the new incentives provided to U.S.- and foreign-based companies. The unfavorable treatment of foreign investment will weaken the dollar, promoting U.S. exports and discouraging imports. The short-term effect on repatriated earnings is the opposite.

Other Business Sectors

The new law also rearranges tax burdens substantially outside of manufacturing. Domestic trade and service businesses are generally among those with the largest direct tax reductions. Again, these sectors generally benefit from rate reduction more than they lose from base broadening. Tax reductions for the trade sector will be offset significantly in the first few years, however, as the new installment sale and inventory capitalization rules apply retroactively to existing receivables and inventories.

Long-term contractors will be required to pay tax earlier under a composite accounting method that requires at least 40 percent of a contract to be reported on the percentage-of-completion method and calls for interest to be paid by the taxpayer to the extent that this 40 percent method is shown to have resulted in deferral of tax during the contract. Contractors will also be more susceptible to the minimum tax, which requires use of the percentage-of-completion method in the computation of alternative minimum taxable income. Builders of commercial and multi-family real estate who have used a completed-contract method will have both higher costs and reduced demand due to slower depreciation allowances and provisions aimed against tax shelters.

Public utilities will also face generally higher taxes due to the repeal of the investment tax credit, of which they have been among the most intensive users, and a general slowdown of depreciation allowances. Gas and electric utilities will have depreciable lives for most assets extended for five years with no acceleration of method. Telecommunications will fare relatively better than the others, having persuaded Congress that rapidly changing technology justifies much shorter depreciable lives for many telephone assets. In the rate-regulated sector, the key issue is how rate commissions will respond to the reduction in tax rates, which forgives deferred taxes, at the same time that future taxes are raised by repeal of the investment tax credit and broadening of the tax base. It is likely that rates will eventually be higher because of the new tax rules.

In the transportation industries, trucking has clearly benefited more than air and rail. Truck-tractor units are the only transportation assets that are allowed more rapid depreciation under the new law, while aircraft, railroad track, and vessels all have slower depreciation. The cost advantage of acquiring aircraft, locomotives, and rolling stock through leasing may also be impaired by the application of passive loss rules or the corporate alternative minimum tax to many lessors.

Overall Sectoral Effects

Within the corporate sector, the various tax changes generally move toward equalizing the taxation of income wherever it originates. To the extent that this leveling is enforced by the alternative minimum tax, it comes at a heavy price in terms of added complexity and uncertainty. Some differentials remain and a few new ones are introduced. Still, after the difficult transitions and adjustments are made, corporate rate reduction and base broadening mean that investment and pricing will be influenced less by taxes, with consequent improvements in efficiency.

At the same time, the burden on corporate business has been increased relative to that on noncorporate business, the nonprofit sector, and labor income. This increase adds to the tax bias against the use of capital, especially in the predominantly corporate manufacturing sector of the economy.

Adjusting to the new reality   Those who would change the tax law are always faced with the dilemma that any improvements must be bought at the price of disruptions and dislocations during the ensuing transition. Taxes become capitalized into the values of property. Changes in tax law result in windfall gains and losses as these capital values change. Changes that create losses are often criticized as "retro-active."

Traditionally, tax law writers have taken care to minimize the windfall losses by means of general transition rules that either grandfather the old tax rules until property changes hands or phase in the new provisions to slow down the market adjustments. At the same time, windfall gains are not only allowed but speeded up if possible to maximize the political appeal. The problem in this tax reform effort was the revenue neutrality constraint. Transition rules would have delayed the revenue increases, making a revenue-neutral bill impossible unless the benefits were also postponed. Consequently, Congress chose in many cases to forgo the usual transition protection for existing properties. The passive loss limitations, investment interest limits, repeal of the capital gains exclusion, many of the new foreign tax rules, and elements of the minimum tax have all been applied with minimal transition relief. While the political motivation is understandable, the harsh transition raises serious issues of fairness. Also, the precedent will surely increase investor uncertainty about relying on any current tax law.

Adjustment to the new tax law will include changes in the ownership of property as well as changes in sectoral costs and demands. In addition to shifts from individual to corporate ownership and vice versa, there will be shifts in the prospective tax benefits of leasing equipment, looked at from both sides of the transaction. Current lessors may find themselves subject to the alternative minimum tax because of the depreciation and book preferences combined with low reported profits due to leverage. Corporations with a persistent alternative minimum tax position are at a cost disadvantage (other things being equal) as lessors when compared with those not subject to minimum tax. While the tax benefits of leasing are generally lower than before, due to rate reduction and the loss of the investment tax credit, there is a new category of prospective lessees, namely corporations facing minimum tax. Corporations with net operating loss carryovers will continue to have an incentive to lease, although such cases will be fewer under a broader income definition.

The urge to merge has been somewhat aided by tax consider-ations under old law. Lower rates, repeal of the General Utilities rule, and the reduced prospect of artificial tax losses will take away some of this motivation. At the same time, some new merger opportunities may result from a desire to avoid the minimum tax by acquiring companies with relatively little pref-erence income.

Two very important and related accomplishments have been achieved in the new tax bill. These are the narrowing of differentials in the taxation of income among corporate businesses and the reduction in rates, which itself reduces the size of the remaining distortions.

The accomplishments of tax reform come with a number of disappointments and failed opportunities. The new law moves away from, rather than toward, the integration and equalization of the corporate and individual taxes. It sacrifices fairness by giving retroactive effect to many provisions for the sake of short-term revenues. It introduces some unnecessarily complex new provisions—the corporate alternative minimum tax and foreign tax credit limitations, in particular—that will involve costly compliance and difficult enforcement.

Any legislation is inevitably a compromise. The ultimate judgment is not whether it is close to perfect, but whether, all things considered, it is better than the law it replaces. In my judgment, the new tax law is better, but barely.

Comments by Charls E. Walker

ALTHOUGH I agree with almost everything Larry Dildine has said in this paper, I cannot agree with his conclusion. The Tax Reform Act of 1986 is not, on balance, good legislation. It is not true reform in the sense of providing a better tax system overall than the previous one. I would be extremely disheartened by this, except that I do not consider the 1986 act the last chapter in U.S. tax policy. If viewed instead as a building block for truly fundamental tax reform in the years ahead—that is, a shift toward consumption taxes—the act can be considered worthwhile.

My attitudes toward the new law are mixed. The lower marginal rates for individuals and corporations are important and much to be desired; I only hope they will be implemented on schedule. But the manner in which these rates are to be paid for—through sharply higher taxes on business activity—constitutes policy error of the first order.

One major reason for disliking the tax reform act is not for itself but because congressional concentration on it prevented a frontal attack on the nation's sky-high federal budget deficit. Systematic attempts to reduce the federal deficit were in effect crowded out. If it is true, as most economists believe, that the deficit is the primary cause of the nation's massive trade imbalance, and if in turn the large excess of imports over exports of manufactured goods is the basic cause of near stagnation in the industrial sector, then it follows that, to the extent tax reform has taken center stage, industry has suffered significantly. The major blame, by the way, for inaction on the deficit—especially the unwillingness to support a badly needed tax increase—lies with the administration, not Congress. A president who carried forty-nine of fifty states in his reelection campaign, and who had put budget balance in the forefront of his original campaign promises, could have been expected to lead a successful fight in 1985 and 1986 to restore soundness to federal fiscal affairs. Ronald Reagan's failure to do so will be judged by history, and that judgment will be severe. (Politically, he is already paying a price through a shift of control in the Senate that resulted at least in part from the trade deficit and industrial stagnation.)

A second failure of the tax reform act is that it will result in a $120 billion increase in corporate taxes in the next five years. Corporations whose taxes will rise complain that the increase would not be so bad if the additional revenues went to reduce the federal deficit; but to raise business taxes simply to cut individual taxes at a time like this is outrageous public policy.

Those who sold the legislation as a $120 billion tax cut for individuals ought to be ashamed. Everyone knows that corporations do not really pay taxes. They are ultimately passed on to corporation owners, workers, and customers, with no net tax reduction for individuals, although just who gets hit and for how much by this hidden tax is unknown, a situation true tax reformers should surely abhor. And, of course, higher business taxes raise the cost of doing business and risk pushing an already sluggish economy into recession. Indeed, most econometric models forecast a decline below baseline in real growth in the first few years under the new law.

With respect to the popular political sport of penalizing corporations, which do not vote, while pandering to individuals, who do vote, tax reform is simply another chapter in overall 1980s tax policy. Between 1981 and 1991 federal tax measures enacted thus far will raise corporate taxes by $39 billion in 1986 dollars while cutting individual taxes a whopping $1.5 trillion.

Increases in business taxes during a period of slow growth are bad enough; to concentrate them so sharply on saving and investment in a low-saving economy that is finding it difficult to sustain its international competitiveness compounds the error. The United States is a high-wage economy competing with low-wage economies abroad. If it is to compete in such a manner as to maintain or enhance living standards here, as opposed to simply depreciating its currency, productivity must increase at a strong and steady rate. This will require maximum investment in state-of-the art machinery and equipment. Under these conditions higher taxes on such investments make little sense.

But the act does raise such taxes, and with a vengeance. Consider these findings by the Bureau of Economic Analysis of the Department of Commerce: at a combined discount and inflation rate of only 8 percent, the new law will raise the effective tax rate on returns to research and experimentation equipment from 7 to 37 percent, on computer equipment from −9 to 37 percent, on instruments from −5 to 31 percent, and on general industrial equipment from −5 to 28 percent.

Although some income tax purists argue that all investment income should be taxed the same—competitive considerations are of course neglected—the only sensible and fair approach to taxing investment is to permit first-year expensing. This would help avoid double taxation of saving. It would also foster the investment needed for international competitiveness. But these reasons aside, few people of pragmatic bent would argue that taxes on productive investment should be increased sharply at this particular time.

I would be unhappy indeed if I thought the Tax Reform Act of 1986 marked the last chapter in U.S. tax reform, but it will not. Past tax reform movements have shown a definite rhythm. In 1969, 1976, and 1986, closing loopholes and broadening the tax base carried the day; in 1978 and 1981, saving, investment, and capital formation were the battle cry. Base broadening won out when times were good and taxpayers had become disgusted with what they perceived to be the unfairness of the system. Encouraging saving and investment took precedence when the economy was not performing up to expectations and growth in living standards lagged.

The pendulum will swing back, perhaps sooner than expected. A full-fledged recession in 1987 or 1988 could lead to early restoration or replication of some investment incentives eliminated by the 1986 reforms, perhaps supplemented by a broad-based consumption tax that could help cut federal deficits. If in that process the lower marginal rates of the 1986 reforms are sustained, then by the 1990s the United States could have a tax system truly suited to the highly competitive world of the twenty-first century.

Comments by Charles R. Hulten

THE IMPACT of rising tax burdens on capital formation is one of the most controversial aspects of tax reform. The tax reform act eliminates many important investment incentives—the investment tax credit is the best example—and thereby shifts approximately $120 billion in tax liability from individuals to corporations. Some see this as a major threat to U.S. economic growth and international competitiveness.

How much credence should be given to this point of view? Larry Dildine has given us an examination of the industrial effects of the tax reform act. I will complement his remarks by examining tax reform from the perspective of formal growth analysis.

Growth analysts typically identify three factors as contributing to aggregate economic growth: capital, labor, and technical progress, or, more precisely, the efficiency with which capital and labor are transformed into output. The growth rate of output is the sum of these three factors: the growth rate of capital, multiplied by capital's effect on output growth (which can be shown to equal its share in total income); the growth rate of labor input, multiplied by its income share; and the residual growth in output not explained by the first two factors, which is associated with technical change. This last effect is often termed "multifactor productivity."

Data from the Bureau of Labor Statistics (BLS) indicate that the private business sector of the U.S. economy grew at an average rate of 3.2 percent a year over the period from 1948 to 1985. These data also show that 19 percent of this was due to the growth in labor input, 38 percent was due to capital formation, and 43 percent was due to improvements in multifactor productivity. In the manufacturing sector, multifactor productivity explained 56 percent of the growth in real output.[4]

BLS data thus lead to the conclusion that multifactor productivity was the most important source of U.S. economic growth over the post–World War II period. This conclusion is, if anything, an understatement. My own research shows that much of the observed capital formation over this period was actually due to productivity growth; when this feedback effect is taken into account, multifactor productivity accounts for almost all postwar growth.[5]

It should also be noted that variations in economic growth are closely tied to variations in multifactor productivity. From 1948 to 1973, the output of the U.S. business sector grew at an average

4. U.S. Department of Labor, Bureau of Labor Statistics, *Trends in Multifactor Productivity, 1948–81,* Bulletin 2178 (Washington, D.C.: Government Printing Office, 1982).

5. Charles R. Hulten, "On the Importance of Technical Change," *American Economic Review,* vol. 69 (March 1979), pp. 126–35.

annual rate of 3.6 percent; from 1973 to 1981, this rate fell to 2.3 percent. This collapse was due almost entirely to the decline in the growth rate of multifactor productivity. Virtually the same is true of the manufacturing sector.

These estimates provide a framework for discussing the potential effects of tax reform on economic growth. It is apparent from the discussion above that multifactor productivity, not capital formation, is the most important source of growth. Only a fraction of our historical growth rate is at risk from tax policies that discourage capital formation. Much the same can be said of most industries in the business sector.

How big an adverse effect might one expect? This is hard to predict, as Dildine's paper shows. However, Jane Gravelle has estimated the impact on marginal effective tax rates of eliminating the investment tax credit, establishing the new depreciation system, cutting the corporate and individual statutory income tax rates, and subjecting capital gains to full income tax rates. She estimates that the cost of capital will increase by 7 percent for nonresidential structures and by 13 percent for producers' durable equipment, or by approximately 10 percent for structures and equipment combined.[6]

If one assumes that a $1 increase in the cost of capital translates into a proportionate decline in the demand for capital, the desired stock of capital will be 10 percent lower as a result of tax reform. (This assigns a rather large impact to tax policy; recent estimates by Harper and Gullickson for the manufacturing sector suggest that a 1 percent increase in the cost of capital will lower the demand for capital by only 0.42 percent.)[7] If one assumes further that saving effects can be ignored, the lower demand for capital translates directly into lower capital formation and real GNP growth.[8] The reduction in output is approximately equal to the change in capital multiplied by capital's share of income. Since the BLS estimates that the income share of structures and equip-

6. Jane G. Gravelle, "Effective Corporate Tax Rates in the Major Tax Revision Plans: A Comparison of the House, Senate, and Conference Committee Versions," Congressional Research Service, Report 86-854E, August 26, 1986.

7. Michael J. Harper and William Gullickson, "Cost Functions Models and Accounting for Growth in U.S. Manufacturing, 1949–83," U.S. Department of Labor, Bureau of Labor Statistics, December 1986.

8. I ignore the impact of tax reform on the supply of saving because it is difficult to estimate, and the link between saving and investment is tenuous in an economy open to international trade and international capital flows. Furthermore, the future supply of saving is much more likely to be dominated by the size of the federal budget deficit than by tax considerations.

ment is approximately 23 percent, the 10 percent reduction in these types of capital will lower future output by 2.4 percent.

Over what time horizon will this change take place? Investment decisions take time to implement, and if the reduced demand for depreciable capital is spread over four years, real output will be reduced by approximately 0.6 percent a year over this period. But after that, the growth rate of GNP is not affected, since a one-time change in tax incentives will not, in general, permanently alter the rate of growth.

These estimates are extremely rough and ignore much of the complexity of tax reform. They ignore, for example, the potential benefit of lower nominal interest rates. They also ignore the positive effect on the cost of capital for inventories and land, which Gravelle estimates will fall by about 19 percent and which, under the procedure used above, should add about 0.25 percent to the growth rate of real GNP. They do, however, serve to indicate the order of magnitude of the negative impact on capital formation and lead to the conclusion that it is neither very large nor permanent.

Judging from the BLS estimates, the principal concern should be the impact of tax reform on multifactor productivity, the most important source of economic growth. This is, however, even more difficult to assess than the impact on capital formation, because multifactor productivity is measured as a residual and thus includes such disparate factors as technical and organizational change, changes in the quality and utilization rates of capital and labor, changes in allocational efficiency, and pure measurement error. Consequently, no clear link exists between changes in tax policy and productivity change.

Most discussions of this issue do attempt to link tax policy to productivity change via the effects on R&D spending. This is a tenuous link, at best, since R&D spending is almost certain to be more heavily influenced by innovation possibilities than by tax benefits. Furthermore, the link between R&D spending and multifactor productivity growth is hard to establish. Nevertheless, it may be worth noting that the principal tax benefit for R&D spending is not disturbed by tax reform: intangible costs, including R&D, can still be written off immediately, rather than being depreciated. And the R&D tax credit lives on, though at a slightly lower rate. The full taxation of capital gains may create a disincentive for younger high-technology firms, but the overall lowering of statutory tax rates should make the prospect of successful innovation even more attractive.

On the negative side, a lower rate of investment may reduce the rate of innovation because capital embodies much new technology. However, tax changes affect marginal investment, and investment that embodies new technology is unlikely to be of marginal profitability. Furthermore, if embodiment of new technology in capital really is an important factor in determining the rate of productivity growth, the decline in multifactor productivity growth noted above should have been accompanied by a decline in capital formation, but it was not.

On the other hand, positive productivity can be expected from an improved allocation of resources, a point emphasized in Dildine's paper. Gravelle's estimates suggest a leveling of effective tax rates within the corporate sector; and the general compression of statutory tax rates, together with the assault on tax shelters, suggests a significant reduction in tax distortions. Also, the general lowering of statutory tax rates will tend to reduce the size of remaining distortions and lessen the effect of taxes on economic decisions.

As usual, the benefit from reducing tax-induced distortions is hard to quantify precisely, but Fullerton and Mackie put the number between $28 and $352 billion a year.[9] Applying my previous assumptions to the middle of this range results in an equivalent increase in growth of 0.05 percent. Thus, on balance, it is likely that tax reform will have a positive impact on the growth rate of multifactor productivity in the U.S. private business sector.

The same can be said of labor input, which will probably be stimulated by the lower marginal tax rate on money wages. According to the evidence cited by Henry Aaron in this volume, the impact on output is likely to be small—perhaps about 0.16 percent a year, using (somewhat inappropriately) the four-year phase-in assumption adopted for capital.

This analysis leads me to the conclusion that tax reform will not have a strong effect on growth, either positive or negative. Adding up my very rough estimates yields a slightly negative effect of 0.14 percentage points a year for the first four years and no effect thereafter. This estimate corresponds rather closely to the results of Fullerton and Mackie, who, using a different approach, obtain a long-run change in output ranging from −0.4 percent to +0.2 percent.

9. Don Fullerton, Yolanda K. Henderson, and James Mackie, "Investment Allocation and Growth under the Tax Reform Act of 1986," U.S. Department of the Treasury, Office of Tax Analysis, December 1986.

Some industries will, of course, bear a heavier burden than others: those industries, like real estate, that were associated with the use of tax shelters, and capital-intensive industries that benefited from the investment tax credit will tend to lose relative to other industries, like those producing high-technology products or using high-technology processes.

In sum, it seems fair to conclude that the other benefits of tax reform will not be purchased at the expense of aggregate long-run growth.

Comments by Dean P. Phypers

In 1984 and 1985, I worked on the Committee for Economic Development's Tax Policy Subcommittee. Although even after many months of work the subcommittee members remained unable to agree on a great many specifics, we did hammer out a set of principles against which we agreed a tax code should be measured. These were published in October 1985 in a statement titled *Tax Reform for a Productive Economy*. Against this set of criteria a report card on the new tax law would show "passing" but hardly "honors."

Simply lowering rates has gone a long way toward diminishing the effect of economic distortions under the previous law, although many still remain. Progress was made in moderating the use of the tax code to allocate resources among industrial sectors, which should ultimately result in greater economic efficiency. Progress was also made in providing more equal tax treatment of income from similar sources.

In contrast to the modest gains it represents, however, this law does not well serve principles of accountability or stability and does not mitigate the effects of inflation on the tax burden borne by individual taxpayers. Neither is the law simpler than before for corporations. Finally, the competitive position of the United States and the world economy did not get a great deal of attention in putting this bill together. It is this last oversight that I would like to discuss further.

Broadly speaking, the law's effects on America's ability to compete are mixed. The cost of capital for productive equipment has been increased by this legislation, and Larry Dildine has commented on this point. There is at least a short-term offset in that the United States has considerable capacity in place, much of it relatively new. The export income from this capacity will be taxed at a lower rate than it is for many of our competitors. In addition, as Dildine has commented, many multinational companies will have an excess of foreign tax credits to offset domestic taxes. This should result in real net savings in the worldwide tax bill of those multinationals.

The relative advantage will be short term because some of America's trading partners have already begun to alter their tax structures in response to the new law, and the matter is under study in Germany and Japan. However, even when this local adjustment takes place, the relative advantage of reduced rates in foreign markets may well be more to our benefit than it is to local companies. This is because such characteristics as dividend relief in Germany and the debt-oriented capital structure in Japan have already given local companies a tax advantage over multinationals. Therefore, their relative gain in any local tax rate reduction will be less. (I would like to add one caveat to the point Dildine made that foreign companies investing in the United States will see their tax bills increase as a result of the changes in the U.S. tax law. This can be expected to be true in the aggregate, but if, for example, U.S. high-tech companies find the new tax law to be beneficial, so will competitive foreign high-tech companies.)

Other provisions in the law also affect the ability of the United States to compete. The overall limitation on foreign tax credits was retained after considerable debate. The provision still allows for averaging high-taxed and low-taxed foreign operating income, but now there are many separate provisions eliminating low-taxed passive income from the averaging mechanism. This results in considerable loss of flexibility for some multinationals. Although I expect a great deal of restructuring to take place in the service industries in response to the new law, those industries that have significant physical capital investments in foreign countries will not have the flexibility to reposition their investments. Therefore, they will see their costs increase and, of course, any increase in costs hurts our competitive posture.

As a more positive result of the new law, the addition of more precise and uniform rules regarding foreign currency transactions should reduce the amount of nonproductive game playing in such transactions and could even help stabilize currency markets.

On the purely negative side, the new law increases the complexity and cost of compliance with the tax code without necessarily providing a commensurate revenue gain for the Treasury. Recently, the tax officer of a major multinational corporation told me in frustration that he was going to return to private practice because compliance for his corporation would be impossible.

The introduction of the concept of a "super royalty," which requires multinationals to include in their U.S. taxable income amounts that are commensurate with the income attributable to intangible properties originated in the United States, allows the Internal Revenue Service retrospectively to readjust an otherwise arm's-length contractual royalty relationship. This is a meat-cleaver approach to a problem requiring surgery with a scalpel. The logic of this provision is obscure, and no apparent attention was given to the practicalities of administration and the potential reactions of taxing authorities in other countries. It will certainly not help the competitive position of the United States.

The methodology for allocating expenses for interest and research and development to offset foreign income also resulted from a cavalier legislative process. Here again, the logic is obscure, and the resulting loss of deductions will both increase costs for international companies and militate against research and development investment in this country.

The foreign tax credit limitations on dividends of minority-owned subsidiaries or joint ventures also pose a potentially negative influence on U.S. competition in world markets. The United States must focus on export markets and foreign investment if it is to resolve its balance of trade problems. Considering the constraints on investment in foreign markets, joint ventures of various types may be the most viable means of resolving those problems. Singling out such ventures for punitive tax treatment is counterproductive.

Reductions in de minimus exceptions for special treatment of passive income will create a significant compliance burden and cause nuisance adjustments. This sort of thing does not serve the cause of simplicity; instead, it frustrates the progress that has been made in tax theory.

Despite these criticisms, however, the legislation is on the whole somewhat more effective than Dildine suggests, although this may be mostly a matter of judgment.

First, I would expect the improvement in economic efficiency over time to be somewhat better than anticipated. Second, in regard to the swapping of assets, I would not expect to see a great movement of passive investments to corporate form unless they were soundly based economically. The other kinds of moves, the Christmas Eve specials put together for highly questionable, highly leveraged, tax-only reasons, will die of their own accord—and good riddance. Third, I believe the second- and third-level effects that Dildine describes will ameliorate the effects of the new law on various industries much more than is presently believed.

One has only to attend a few tax planning sessions to see how creatively industry is already beginning to deal with the new law.

Finally and most important, the new law provides a much better basic structure from which to meet tomorrow's challenges. Perhaps foremost among these is the budget deficit. Whereas reduction of expenditures should be the primary thrust in reducing the deficit, I do not know how we can adequately address the problem without ultimately raising revenue. The tax structure we now have in place, provided we are willing to keep its fundamental concepts intact, is a better base from which to raise revenue than we have had, whether we do so by changing rates or by adding consumption taxes.

Whatever changes we make in the future, I would hope that the objective of improving the competitive posture of the United States becomes a much better recognized and much more thoughtfully considered objective than it has been.

Effects on Financial Decisionmaking

EUGENE STEUERLE

NUMEROUS tax bills have been enacted over the last three decades, each one promoted as a means of encouraging and fostering economic growth. In that sense, the Tax Reform Act of 1986 is little different from past legislation. Previously, however, encouraging growth through the tax code primarily meant providing fiscal stimulus by reducing taxes. Sometimes investment and saving incentives were offered if a portion of the revenue lost through lower taxes was designated to subsidize purchases of assets by either businesses or individuals. Attempts to redesign or eliminate programs in the tax code, on the other hand, were disdained as institutional, structural, or microeconomic tinkering that was unimportant compared with the basic goal of providing stimulus to the economy.

This fiscal approach to economic policy actually worked well at times. When the ratio of public debt to GNP was declining and bracket creep was steadily increasing tax burdens, tax reduction was a reasonable means of offsetting fiscal drag without any real threat that the policy would later have to be reversed. Similarly, as inflation raised the effective tax rate on depreciable capital, some adjustments in tax policy were justified to encourage investment.

The application of this type of tax policy to almost all economic situations, however, was doomed to fail for two reasons. First, the nation could not always be perceived as going into a recession, being in a recession, or just coming out of a recession. Such perceptions of the economy created continual demands for further stimulus. Second, the tendency to ignore issues of tax design eventually resulted in an accumulation of problems—call them institutional or technical, if you will—that became more than minor in their aggregate effect on the economy.

The dilemma of fiscal and tax policymakers was not very

The author wishes to thank Larry Dildine, John Makin, and David Shakow for suggestions and comments.

different from that facing monetary authorities. The money supply could not be accelerated continually, even if acceleration was viewed as a means of providing stimulus to the economy. Once the boost given by one acceleration had ended, monetary authorities were faced with the unhappy choice of deceleration later.

In a similar manner, whether the argument for a tax reduction was Keynesian or supply side in orientation, once one cut was made, another was supposedly needed. Once the country moved into an era in which the public debt was rising relative to GNP, however, it became almost impossible to avoid confronting the fact that further fiscal stimulus would have to be offset later by a contractionary policy. Likewise, once so-called saving and investment incentives led to negative tax rates for many types of transactions, especially when significant amounts of debt were involved, additional saving and investment incentives became less feasible as stimulative policy options. Moreover, whatever the short-term beneficial effects of past incentives, their poor design meant that the country still suffered large long-term costs.

The latest round of tax reform is unique. Since the act aims at revenue neutrality, it forgoes the usual stimulus through tax reduction. Moreover, rather than provide further tax reduction for certain purchases or deposits, the act actually eliminates many inefficient or ineffective incentives.

How, then, can this type of tax reform increase growth? The growth comes from dealing with the very institutional, structural, and micro issues that were previously thought to be of secondary importance. Structural reform stimulates growth not by increasing the supply of funds, but by encouraging a more efficient flow of those funds.

An optimistic assessment

While my previous role makes it difficult for me to render an unbiased judgment,[1] my overall assessment of the Tax Reform Act of 1986 is that on balance it is good for the economy. It will not stop recessions, but it was not designed to stop recessions. It will have significant effects on financial flows in the short run, but its main effects will appear in the long run in more efficient use of human and capital resources.

Government encourages long-term growth by freeing individual workers and investors to develop their productive capacity to the fullest and by encouraging the development of financial

---

1. The author was the economic staff coordinator in charge of the original coordination and design of the tax reform study known as Treasury I.

institutions that help move funds efficiently from savers to investors. Despite some unnecessary complications, the new tax act does free individuals to make their economic and financial decisions with much less attention to tax consequences. The tax code is going to be less constraining an influence on billions of decisions made by tens of millions of taxpayers. This shift is already evident in the financial markets. Portfolio managers, brokers, and even tax shelter salesmen are all emphasizing that new financial investments should be valued primarily on the basis of their economic merit. This change in financial incentives and behavior will improve the allocation of capital in the economy.

The reform deals with a wide variety of technical issues that I believe to be collectively important, although of lesser consequence taken one by one. As an example, the supply of loanable funds to entrepreneurs with productive ideas has increased simply because loans are less valuable to those who borrow against pension, life insurance, and individual retirement accounts; and private borrowers will find it more difficult to persuade state and local officials to issue tax-exempt securities on their behalf. In my organization of the original Treasury effort, I tried to direct attention to such small issues by presenting a comprehensive list of options. The goal was to put on the table almost all the ways in which the old code resulted in disparate taxation of income, depending upon its sources and uses. Although I still have reservations about some of the results—for instance, I am bothered by some details of the international tax provisions and the new minimum taxes—Congress did tackle a number of issues and did reduce many disparities.

Policymakers have always had great difficulty dealing with the thousands of policies and programs that, one by one, can be considered minor. In my view, the duplication of programs on both the tax and expenditure side of the budget is responsible for much of the inefficiency of government today and has prevented the development of new policies. The new tax act does not solve this basic problem, but it does move in the right direction. As a result, it puts the country in a better position to respond to future crises and emergencies and to develop efficient long-term tax policies.

A view of the past

I argued above that the new tax code encourages taxpayers to make decisions on the basis of economic considerations rather than on the basis of tax considerations. To see how this conclusion is reached, it is useful to review how the old tax code interacted with other factors to affect saving and investment flows before 1986.

Two nontax factors were of special importance. First, inflation became an expected presence in the economy, sometimes at very high rates. Second, dramatic changes took place in the financial marketplace: flows of interest payments and receipts grew to a large percentage of GNP; the household sector became a major borrower; and innovation allowed professional lawyers, accountants, and traders to quickly arbitrage away discrepancies in rates of return, whether caused by economic circumstances or tax differentials. Indeed, there would have been no major tax reform if it were not for the impact on the tax system of inflation and innovation in financial markets.

As for the old tax code itself, the most important features were high statutory tax rates, the inability to measure income from capital properly in an inflationary environment, and a wide variety of so-called saving and investment incentives. These tax features interacted with inflation and financial innovation to create an incentive structure with the following four characteristics.

—*Very high effective tax rates on some types of income.* Very high effective tax rates, often over 100 percent, applied to certain types of income. Among the most penalized were interest receipts and short-term capital gains. At the high inflation rates of the late 1970s and before enactment of the accelerated cost recovery system, many equity investments in depreciable capital were also penalized.

—*Low or negative effective tax rates on other incomes.* Many other types of investment faced low or negative tax rates. Investment in consumer durables and housing received favorable tax treatment, while saving through pension plans often resulted in zero or negative tax rates on income from capital. At lower rates of inflation, investment credits, combined with accelerated depreciation, could also lead to negative tax rates on equity investments.

—*Low or negative after-tax interest rates.* Negative tax rates often resulted when investments were leveraged. The subsidy for borrowing is equal to the inflation rate times the tax rate. In many years, this subsidy was so large for some taxpayers that their after-tax interest rates were negative. At 8 percent inflation, for instance, a taxpayer in the 50 percent bracket would have had positive real after-tax borrowing costs only if interest rates rose to 16 percent or more.

—*Up-front deductions.* Most types of investment and saving tax incentives allowed taxpayers to take substantial write-offs and deductions soon after assets were purchased. In these early years, the government often turned money over to taxpayers rather than the other way around.

Forms of Tax Arbitrage

This incentive structure had a number of profound effects on the flows of saving and investment in the economy. As I noted earlier, the financial markets have become remarkably adept at taking advantage of differences in rates of return across assets. When these differences are created by tax differentials, the markets encourage tax-motivated transactions known as tax arbitrage.

My research has shown that two conditions are necessary for what I have labeled "normal" tax arbitrage. First, there must be differences in the tax treatment of different assets. Second, different taxpayers, domestic or foreign, must face different tax rates. When those conditions are present, there is an incentive for minimization of taxes through the redistribution of assets. Unlike most other assets, interest-bearing assets are taxed in full upon the entire inflationary component each year. Thus in an inflationary economy the most important tax differential is between interest and other types of returns to capital. This leads to the most common form of normal tax arbitrage, borrowing to purchase assets that are taxed at lower rates than interest income. Almost all leveraged purchases of assets, including houses, commodities, depreciable assets, and farmland, involve tax arbitrage. That is one reason I applied the adjective "normal" to this process.

To complicate the world a bit further, various saving incentives have encouraged what I have labeled "pure" tax arbitrage. Unlike normal tax arbitrage, pure tax arbitrage requires neither the redistribution of assets in society nor taxpayers in different tax brackets. Here tax saving is generated essentially through the simultaneous buying and selling of the same asset. Borrowing to purchase interest-bearing IRA accounts is one example; commodity straddles is another. Pure tax arbitrage, however, complements normal tax arbitrage in encouraging an increase in the amount of borrowing without any necessary increase in either net saving or real investment.

One way of perceiving the importance of both normal and pure tax arbitrage is the following. In 1981, interest recipients paid tax of about $68 billion on interest received, but interest deductions had a value of almost $30 billion more. For a given amount of real investment in the economy, the greater the amount of private borrowing involved, the lower the net amount of taxes collected by the government. Although there is some debate as to who eventually pockets the tax reduction, the net effect is still clear: minimization of total tax burdens can be greatly enhanced through increased leverage in society.

Effects on Flows of Investment and Saving

Among the more obvious effects of this incentive structure were the following. Private debt grew at fairly fast rates. The tax code, of course, was not the only cause of this change. The initial postwar decline in the ratio of public debt to GNP, for instance, helped keep interest rates low and encouraged the substitution of private for public debt. Even when the ratio of public debt to GNP began to increase and real interest rates turned up, however, the ratio of private debt to GNP continued its upward path.

The tax shelter industry grew. Tax shelters were only one reflection of a tax system that for certain investments provided negative tax rates as well as substantial up-front deductions and credits. Corporations often could not take advantage of these tax provisions because they could not pass through to shareholders negative taxable income nor take credits greater than their tax liabilities before credits. The shelter market, therefore, was driven to the individual and partnership sectors, where individuals could use negative taxable income from one business to offset both positive wage income and income from other businesses. As the learning curve expanded, an ever increasing flow of saving began to flow through the shelter markets.

Not only new assets went into the shelter industry. In what I have labeled the disincorporation of America, corporations began to sell off many billions of dollars of assets to partnerships. Of course, the corporate sector often leased back these same assets. In some cases, corporate raiders facilitated this transfer of assets. Many corporations, however, did not need corporate raiders to induce them to minimize tax burdens.

For high-income taxpayers, second homes and farmland also became useful tax shelters. Especially when real after-tax interest rates were low or negative, bidding for these assets tended to increase their price. Low after-tax real interest rates also led to increased bidding for gold and commodities in some years. These were not simply hedges against inflation. The interest costs were deductible, but the inflationary gains in value were deferred from taxation. In the case of farmland, the taxpayer was able to increase consumption by borrowing against the increased value of the assets.

Some effects of this type of tax system were more obvious than others. In the financial markets, a movement in the price of one asset because of a tax preference tends to be reflected in a change in the value of other assets. For instance, over the postwar period there has been a strong negative correlation between the real change in value of the stock market and the real change in value of land, residential structures, and nonresidential plant and equipment (mainly structures). Thus some of the relative price changes of the 1970s—large increases in the value of land and poor stock market performance—were partially tax induced.

The efficiency effects were equally as serious, if less obvious. When some assets are tax-preferred, investment in assets with less than maximum productivity is encouraged. At the extreme, investment in unproductive assets can actually become profitable when one of two conditions holds: the effective tax rate on equity-financed investments is negative, or the after-tax real rate of interest is negative. There are many examples of both household and business investments that were clearly unproductive: windmill farms, empty commercial office buildings, and many seldom-used or seldom-rented vacation homes. This type of investment was harmful to the economy as a whole, mainly because better economic investment was deterred. In effect, the tax code helped to prevent financial intermediaries from allocating scarce saving to its most productive investment uses.

The old law also created other types of inefficiencies. The highest tax rates often were paid by the most dynamic and successful firms. Thus an innovative firm often paid tax at a 46 percent rate while another firm was effectively paying a zero or negative tax rate on many of its investments. Since risky investments are often likely to generate the highest rates of return, the tax code tended to encourage safer, less growth-oriented ventures.

In addition, the old law discriminated heavily against new firms and certain older firms that had not been profitable for a number of years. For a given marginal investment, these firms paid higher tax rates than established firms. Only the latter had enough taxable income from other sources to make use of the credits and accelerated allowances allowed under the law. Because new firms were thereby required to achieve a much higher-than-normal rate of return, domestic competition was reduced, and established domestic firms probably made less effort to adopt new technologies and seek new markets.

The impact of the 1986 act   The Tax Reform Act of 1986 did not solve all the problems of the old tax code, but it had an important impact on almost all of them. Its beneficial effects do not derive from some of the well-publicized provisions such as minimum taxes, passive loss rules, and rules that tie sources of borrowing to uses of funds. Instead, the positive impact of the act derives mainly from the reduction in rates of taxation, the elimination of negative tax rates on investment in certain forms of physical capital, and the greater equalization of tax rates among assets without regard to the sources or uses of funds.

I stated above that investment in unproductive capital can occur when tax rates on equity investment or after-tax real interest rates are negative. Because the new act has eliminated the investment credit, investment incentives are now provided mainly in the form of acceleration of deductions. Thus the effective tax rate applying to new equity investments must be positive no matter what the rate of acceleration or the rate of inflation. Hence, the first condition for unproductive investment can no longer be met. As for the second condition, after-tax real interest rates can still become negative, but lower tax rates significantly reduce that probability. The top individual tax rate is now 33 percent, not 50 percent. When taxpayers were in the 50 percent bracket, if the inflation rate was 5 percent, the interest rate had to be above 10 percent to raise their after-tax real interest rate above zero. At the lower tax rate of 33 percent, the nominal interest rate need only be higher than 7.5 percent.

These provisions then move a long way toward reestablishment of a market where investment dollars are channeled to the most economic and productive uses. To make an after-tax profit today, investors must seek at least some economic reward other than tax relief. No longer are low-risk, unproductive investments likely to be profitable on the basis of tax considerations alone.

The lower tax rates and the reduction in the value of up-front deductions and credits will affect flows of funds in other ways as well.

—Old-style tax shelters simply are no longer viable. The tax shelter industry has been turned around so much that positive economic returns are an important component of almost all investment sales pitches today.

—Differentials among types of investment have been narrowed significantly, and any tax saving from asset shifts and borrowing is much less likely to compensate for the transactions costs that might be involved with more complicated types of tax arbitrage transactions. As a result, many investors will be led to invest their funds directly into corporate stock or in low-cost intermediaries such as banks or mutual funds.

—Corporations will engage less in the sales of tax-preferred assets and there will be fewer leveraged partnership shelters. (Some new incentives for disincorporation have now been created, however, as will be discussed below.)

—Farmland and expensive second homes will be less valuable as shelters to higher-income taxpayers.

—In terms of cash flow within the corporate sector, a greater portion of after-tax dollars will flow to dynamic and successful firms that generate high rates of return on their activities. Returns on risky ventures will now be taxed at 34 percent rather than 46 percent, so that after-tax rewards will increase by almost 22 percent.

—Some, but not all, of the discrimination against new firms will be eliminated. (A typical piece of equipment will still yield insufficient returns in the early years to allow full use of available deductions.) This narrowing of the tax differential between new and established businesses will reduce barriers to entry and should lead to an increase in the number of new businesses or at least improved efficiency of existing firms.

—Lower tax rates raise both the after-tax rate of return for holding interest-bearing assets and the after-tax rate of payment on debt. These changes will reduce both demand and supply for interest-bearing assets and should reduce the interest rate. Much of this decline may already have taken place, although I believe that real interest rates are currently above their long-term equilibrium levels.

—The change in the tax laws may have led to an increase in the value of the stock market. For high-bracket taxpayers, the lower rates reduce the value of noncorporate investment, especially leveraged investment, in land and real estate. As noted, the markets tend to show a negative correlation between stock prices and the prices of land and structures, either residential or nonresidential.

—Limitations on passive loss write-offs, although poorly designed in many respects, force individuals into a corporate type of world where losses can be used only to offset gains from the same basic source of income. These rules will reinforce other changes that encourage taxpayers to invest more directly in corporate stock.

Reduction in Tax Arbitrage Opportunities

Once the impact of lower interest rates works through the system, I also expect the private demand for loans to decrease or at least to slow its rate of increase. This decrease in loan demand will come from a reduction in tax arbitrage opportunities. In the case of pure tax arbitrage, the tax act imposes direct limitations on borrowing from pension and IRA accounts. The act's indirect limitations on normal tax arbitrage opportunities, however, are much more important. Under the new tax law, a much larger percentage of total saving will be concentrated among taxpayers, both individual and corporate, who face an essentially flat marginal tax rate between 28 and 34 percent.[2] Under the old law, a large amount of corporate and individual income was still being taxed at rates above 30–35 percent, indicating that tremendous tax arbitrage opportunities remained to be exploited. The growth in tax shelters reflected this trend. Under the new law the number of available opportunities is greatly reduced.

To see why this change occurs, recall that one of the two necessary conditions for normal tax arbitrage is a difference in tax rates among taxpayers. If most savers are in the same tax bracket, additional lending and borrowing cannot reduce aggregate tax liabilities. Only when taxpayers are in different tax brackets does additional lending from low-bracket savers to high-bracket investors lead to reduced tax collections.

This is not meant to imply that the markets will not continue to sort themselves so that nonpreferred assets are held by remaining low-bracket taxpayers, especially tax-exempt institutions and foreigners. At the margin, however, additional net lending may not reduce taxes further. Moreover, the narrowing of differentials in tax rates may actually cause a one-time reduction in the amount of normal tax arbitrage. Taxpayers may find that the costs of existing tax arbitrage—transactions costs and some loss of diversification—are no longer covered by the tax benefits.

Some Caveats

Like any good economist, I must qualify my conclusions in several respects. First, under the old law, top individual rates were higher than corporate rates; the new law reverses that order. Before, it was especially desirable to move deductions to the individual sector; now, taxable income—in particular, income from nonleveraged equity investments—is given a larger tax preference if it is held in the individual sector. Thus it is unclear whether the trend toward disincorporation will abate, although the new type of disincorporation involves the movement of highly

2. I am grateful to David Shakow for pointing out the reduction in the arbitrage opportunities.

taxable equity to the individual sector. The extent of this shift will depend significantly upon the speed with which the legal community can set up partnerships with corporate characteristics and upon the ability of the financial sector to create liquid markets for these partnership shares. In my view, Congress would likely stop any significant hemorrhage.

Second, while the new law probably reduces the overall growth rate of private borrowing, there is likely to be a shift in the borrowing taking place in different sectors. Since deductions are more valuable in the corporate sector, I expect that a greater share of borrowing will tend to move to that sector.

Third, as for the total amount of private borrowing, a number of forces still encourage debt over equity. Most important are the remaining double taxation of income earned by corporations and the insurance provided to ultimate savers when they hold their assets in interest-bearing deposits at federally insured financial institutions.

Fourth, any change in interest rates depends not just on the tax reform act, but also on overall macroeconomic policy. Real interest rates are greatly dependent on fiscal policy and the related change in the ratio of public debt to GNP. Monetary policy also has a significant effect on interest rates, and the effects of tax policy and monetary policy cannot be separated. Thus the ability of monetary authorities to lower interest rates recently has been facilitated by the Tax Reform Act of 1986. Moreover, monetary authorities will be influenced in the future by the fact that changes in nominal interest rates will now translate more readily into changes in real after-tax interest rates. Thus tax reform has probably resulted in lower interest rates partly through its influence on monetary policy.

Fifth, the new tax code encourages a number of inefficient and unnecessary transactions. There is still an incentive toward mergers, as diversification can greatly reduce the probability of being caught under the minimum tax in any one year. The interest limitation provisions will encourage individuals to reshuffle their loan portfolios, in particular by increasing the amount of their mortgage borrowing relative to other borrowing. Unnecessary sales of homes will also be induced, as deductibility of mortgage interest is dependent in part upon the gross purchase price of the house currently occupied.

Finally, because of the failure to index the measure of capital income for tax purposes, any future increase in inflation will again add to the disparities in the tax treatment of different types of assets and will cause a partial shift back toward the types of markets that existed in the 1970s and early 1980s. Still, the lower tax rates will make the shift less dramatic than in the past.

Summary   Future investment and saving flows will resemble the flows that took place in the 1950s and 1960s in one important respect: financial and real investment decisions will again be based mainly on the economic merit of the assets being purchased. This shift results as much from the reduced rate of inflation as from the changes in the tax code. To argue that the world will be the same again, of course, is to ignore the course of history. New problems and discrepancies have been created by the minimum tax, interest deduction limitations, and other provisions. Still, by returning to the old precept that investments should be guided by economic, not tax, considerations, the 1986 tax act represents a necessary and significant positive step toward the future.

Comments by Robert M. Giordano

IT IS DIFFICULT to quarrel with the description of the general effect of taxes on financial behavior in Eugene Steuerle's analysis. Tax considerations do play a role in decisionmaking and at times even encourage decisions that might not be made solely on pretax economic considerations. However, as a Wall Street economist, I approach the influence of taxes on financial behavior from a different angle, one that makes me generally skeptical about the quantitative significance of tax factors for saving, investment, and the efficiency of resource allocation on a macroeconomic level. The angle leads to a stronger focus on the microeconomic aspects of the impact of tax reform on financial decisions.

On the macroeconomic level, for example, it is true that the deductibility of interest along with high marginal tax rates encourages borrowing and discourages saving. But increasing after-tax returns on savings by lowering marginal tax rates and increasing the after-tax cost of debt by eliminating nonmortgage interest deductibility will not necessarily alter saving and borrowing behavior significantly. After all, there is an equally plausible alternative to the tax subsidy–tax penalty explanation for the history of high levels of borrowing and low levels of saving in the past twenty years. It goes as follows.

Households demand goods and services based on a desired standard of living. But the standard has been too high to achieve solely by consumption out of current income, and people are too impatient to wait for accumulated financial savings. Hence the amount of borrowing rises and the rate of saving falls. As long as current income is sufficient to service debt and social security and other public and private pension plans provide for adequate retirement income, the savings rate rises mainly when households decide not to consume. Although it is probably too strong to say that saving and borrowing are totally insensitive to changes in after-tax returns and costs, history indicates that, unlike consumers in other industrial countries, Americans give up current consumption for future consumption very grudgingly.

Beginning in the early 1970s, real per capita disposable income fell below its 1960–75 trend level; over the last ten years this income shortfall intensified, with actual real income in 1983 falling to only 90 percent of this trend. In a sense, income fell below expectations. But consumption standards, which had been set assuming a continuation of historical trends, were not compromised. Real consumer spending did not consistently deviate much from its trend.

Other information also seems consistent with the idea that tax considerations may play a far smaller role in household financial decisions than Steuerle's analysis implies. For example, the 1983 Federal Reserve Survey of Consumer Finance revealed that only 2 percent of all households owned tax-exempt bonds, with nearly all this ownership concentrated in income brackets greater than $50,000 despite an implied tax rate on municipal bond interest that was well below the 49 percent marginal rate of all municipal bond owners at that time. The survey also found that 60 percent of all families in gross income brackets between $7,500 and $40,000 had an average of $4,300 in consumer credit outstanding, much of it no doubt willingly contracted for at double-digit interest rates. Yet only 22 percent of taxpayers in these brackets deducted nonmortgage interest payments on their income tax returns.

Tax considerations may also play a less-than-expected role for investment in other tax shelters. Admittedly, limited partnership tax shelters have flourished so far in this decade. But a high percentage (35 percent in 1983) report positive ordinary income, suggesting some economic motive for their existence, and not all of the multifamily housing projects and office buildings represent a microeconomic (for example, regional) misallocation of resources, even though on a macroeconomic level the United States now has vacant office space. Some of the vacancies reflect the unexpected depression in certain sectors and regions that previously experienced rapid growth and high absorption of new office and multifamily residential space. Inflation also explains much of the shift into real estate investments over the past ten years. And high inflation, rather than the tax laws, was probably the essential cause of the accelerated use of tax arbitrage.

Because of skepticism toward the so-called benefits from a possibly more efficient allocation of resources, Wall Street identifies with and thinks more about the practical, microeconomic effects of tax reform on financial decisions. Two particularly important impacts of reform are on financial innovations and corporate financial policy.

In terms of financial innovations, tax reform is likely to intensify the issuing of securities to realize cash for holdings of tangible assets. This so-called asset securitization would seem to be encouraged by two provisions of tax reform: the creation of real estate mortgage investment conduits (REMICs) and elimination of the installment sales method of recognizing income on credit sales. REMICs will accelerate the securitization of mortgages because they eliminate many of the shortcomings of current mortgage securitization vehicles that constrain their use. Mortgage securitization was launched initially by the creation of participation certificates (PCs) in mortgage pools. These certificates are undivided interests in a pool of mortgages held by a trust. But the uncertain path of mortgage prepayments, and hence the uncertain average life of a security, creates problems for many investors. The investor takes significant price volatility and reinvestment risks because the instrument effectively changes character as interest rates fluctuate.

In addition, and perhaps more constraining for the use of PCs, it was impossible to achieve passthrough treatment of income (necessary to avoid corporate-level taxation of the trust) if one class of PC owners was paid faster than another or had more default risk. Moreover, if the trust were taxed as a corporation, it could not deduct interest paid because such payments would have to be treated as dividends. To correct these deficiencies, collateralized mortgage obligations (CMOs) were introduced.

CMOs are the debt of the issuer rather than shares in a mortgage pool, and as such, payments to owners can be deducted as interest. This innovation facilitated pricing and allowed maturities to be tailored to institutional needs. However, these securities count as debt on the balance sheet of an issuer, thereby requiring investors to worry about the financial stability of the thrift institution issuing the CMO even though the security of the underlying mortgage may be sound, and the issuer is required to worry about the effect of more debt on his balance sheet. CMOs are thus limited to only the most strongly capitalized institutions. In addition, the income of the issuer is still subject to corporate tax rates, yet losses suffered by the issuer cannot be passed through to CMO owners. These aspects of CMOs created the further risk that the securitization might not be treatable as a sale of collateral. REMICs, on the other hand, allow the creation of multiple-class, mortgage-backed securities that allow income to be treated as a passthrough entity, hence correcting the main deficiencies in PCs and CMOs. With only around 20 percent of $2 trillion in outstanding mortgage debt securitized, the opportunity for growth is enormous.

Tax reform will also enhance the ability to securitize assets by changing the method of accounting for income from installment sales. The new method will allow the sale of receivables without paying concurrent tax on the sale—tax that was previously deferred if receivables were held in a finance subsidiary of the parent company. This innovation could lead to a boom in sales and securitization of receivables such as auto loans or credit card purchases.

Tax reform also encourages another financial innovation: increased use of futures and options. First, reform increases the after-tax return to hedgers and dealers dramatically (44 percent) because futures and options are taxed at ordinary income tax rates that are being reduced from a maximum of 50 percent to 28 percent. Reform also increases the after-tax returns to speculators of using futures (6 percent) because gains and losses are now also taxed at 28 percent instead of the present hybrid 32 percent rate that results from differential taxation of long- and short-term gains. Second, because the declining marginal tax rate of companies increases the after-tax cost of debt, and the cost of issuing debt at the wrong time in an interest rate cycle is thus increased, hedging in the futures and options markets becomes more attractive. Wall Street expects this prospective increase in asset-turnover and hedging-related activity, combined with the reduction in the tax rate on short-term capital gains, to ease whatever pain is inflicted by the abolition of the long-cherished preferential tax treatment on long-term capital gains.

Tax reform could also affect corporate financial policy in both merger and acquisition activities and capital structures. Merger activity could be reduced by repeal of the so-called General Utilities doctrine and the change in treatment of net operating loss carryforwards. The General Utilities doctrine allows an acquiring company to raise the basis of acquired assets for purposes of calculating tax depreciation without recognizing the gain as income yet still allowing depreciation write-offs on the increased value of the assets. Repeal of this provision will significantly raise the price of many acquisitions and thereby reduce the number of mergers, assuming that they are not perfectly price inelastic. It could also reduce the volume of junk bond financing, some of which has been based on this tax provision, thereby increasing the value of junk bonds relative to other securities and enhancing the overall viability of the market. Net operating loss carryforwards of the acquired company can no longer be used without limitation as they can under current law, and this too could restrict some merger activity. Wall Street is hopeful, however, that some of this negative effect may be offset by the enhanced after-tax returns from existing capital relative to new capital and by corporate attempts to avoid the new alternative minimum tax.

The increase in the marginal cost of debt relative to equity implied by tax reform would seem to end the long-term trend of increased leverage in corporate capital structure and increase the role of equity. Because investment banks earn much more on equity underwritings than on straight debt, Wall Street prays this will be so. But such prayers may be wasted. Debt is still much cheaper than equity even though it may become relatively less so with tax reform. Rough calculations suggest that, at current interest rates and stock prices, interest on debt is still about 2 percentage points below the cost of equity under the new law. Moreover, with the declining value of other tax preferences, those companies that previously did not pay taxes will now find debt more attractive. Tax reform may slow the rate of substitution of debt for equity in corporate capital structures (by reducing the attractiveness of mergers, leveraged buyouts, and share repurchases), but it is probably wishful thinking to expect a boom in new equity finance.

Given the complexity of tax reform, how all its nonlinear effects will affect the economy or Wall Street is anyone's guess. But in the end we can probably agree with Steuerle when he says that tax reform takes us in the right direction—that is, as long as it actually turns out to be revenue neutral.

Effects on Real Estate

PATRIC H. HENDERSHOTT
JAMES R. FOLLAIN
DAVID C. LING

THE TAX REFORM ACT of 1986 radically alters the federal income tax system and generally taxes investment activities more heavily. In fact, partial equilibrium analysis leads to the implausible conclusion that tax reform will reduce investment in all capital goods. A more plausible outcome would be reduced investment in relatively disadvantaged capital goods and increased investment in relatively advantaged goods.

The mechanism by which a general decline in investment is converted into a mixed investment response is a fall in interest rates. This fall would follow directly from a general reduction in the demand for investable funds. Allowing for an interest rate decline significantly alters the expected impact of the tax reform act upon real estate. In particular, the negative effect of the act on depreciable real estate will be greatly reduced by an interest rate decline. Moreover, an unfavorable effect on owner-occupied housing shifts to being favorable when a decline in interest rates is incorporated into the analysis.[1]

Provisions and implications for interest rates

Our analysis considers first three classes of provisions of the tax reform act: individual income tax rates, tax depreciation schedules, and investment tax credits. We then discuss the effects these provisions are likely to have on interest rates.

1. This is not the first time the impact of a tax act on real estate has been misunderstood by those who do not allow for interest rate changes. Many observers predicted substantial rent decreases in response to the more generous tax depreciation allowances contained in the Economic Recovery Tax Act of 1981. See, for example, William B. Brueggeman, Jeffrey D. Fisher, and Jerrold J. Stern, "Rental Housing and the Economic Recovery Tax Act of 1981," *Public Finance Quarterly*, vol. 10 (April 1982), pp. 222–41. Hendershott and Shilling, however, foresaw a sharp increase in interest rates as a result of the act and forecast rising real rents. Real rents have, in fact, risen by 10 percent since 1980. Patric H. Hendershott and James Shilling, "The Impacts on Capital Allocation of Some Aspects of the Economic Recovery Tax Act of 1981," *Public Finance Quarterly*, vol. 10 (April 1982), pp. 242–73.

Individual Tax Rate Schedule

The new law replaces the previous fourteen-bracket tax rate schedule with what is best viewed as a four-bracket rate schedule: 15, 28, 33, and 28 percent. The taxable income ranges over which these rates apply are shown for four household types in table 1. The 33 percent marginal rate reverts to 28 percent when a household's *average* tax rate on all income above the standard deduction equals 28 percent. That is, the benefits of the zero tax rate on personal exemptions and of the initial 15 percent tax rate will be phased out for taxpayers with sufficiently high incomes. The phaseout mechanism is a 5 percent surcharge on income above the levels indicated in the table, resulting in a 33 percent marginal rate. The new rate schedule takes effect in 1988 and will be adjusted for inflation beginning in 1989. A transitional tax rate schedule that consists of five tax rates ranging from 11.5 percent to 38.5 percent will be in effect in 1987.

The tax reform act also increases the standard deduction (zero bracket amount) by about one-fourth (to $5,000 in 1988) for married people filing jointly, by a full two-thirds (to $4,400) for heads of household, and by an eighth (to $3,000) for singles. The personal exemption will be increased gradually until 1989, at which time the exemption will equal $2,000 for the taxpayer, the taxpayer's spouse, and dependents. The standard deduction and the personal exemption amounts will be adjusted annually for inflation beginning in 1989 and 1990, respectively. The table on page 73 shows the 1988 income levels at which nonitemizers would have begun paying taxes under the old law (standard deduction plus four, two, two, and one personal exemptions,

Table 1. *Federal Individual Income Tax Rate Schedules, by Taxpayer Status, 1988*
Dollars unless otherwise indicated

	Marginal federal tax rate and taxable income			
Taxpayer status	*15*	*28*	*33*	*28*
Married, joint filers, 2 dependents	0–29,800	29,800–71,900	71,900–192,900	Over 192,900
Married, joint filers, no dependent	0–29,800	29,800–71,900	71,900–171,100	Over 171,100
Household head, 1 dependent	0–23,900	23,900–61,700	61,700–144,600	Over 144,600
Single	0–17,900	17,900–43,200	43,200–100,600	Over 100,600

respectively, for the four households) and will begin paying taxes under the new law. The substantial increases under the new law are expected to remove 6 million taxpayers from the federal income tax rolls.

Taxpayer staus	Old law	New law
Married, joint filers, 2 dependents	8,400	12,800
Married, joint filers, no dependent	6,100	8,900
Household head, 1 dependent	3,800	8,300
Single	3,800	8,300

The reductions in statutory tax rates, including the near doubling of the personal exemption, significantly lower both the average and marginal tax rates at which households will deduct housing expenses. Table 2 contains some sample calculations for households with different adjusted gross incomes. While the calculations are based on numerous specific assumptions, the general result—a cut in these tax rates—holds for virtually all households.

The tax act also alters the tax rate on capital gains income. In 1988 and beyond, the general capital gains exclusion will not exist (in 1987, capital gains will be taxed at no more than a 28 percent tax rate). For most households with significant assets other than consumer durables and their residence, the capital gains rate will be increased from 20 percent or less to 28 or 33 percent. The effective exemption of capital gains taxation on owner-occupied housing continues unaltered, however. That is, capital gains taxation on owner-occupied housing can be postponed upon sale by purchasing another home of at least equal value; in addition, a one-time capital gain of up to $125,000 is excluded from taxation for taxpayers above the age of 55.

Depreciation Schedules

Economists have argued that tax depreciation should equal economic depreciation at replacement cost. This generally means relatively low tax depreciation in the early years of a property but much higher depreciation in later years if significant inflation exists. Because depreciation allowances would be indexed, more than 100 percent (possibly far more) of an asset's value would be deductible over its life. Legislators have not accepted this argument in practice, although they seem to have accepted it in principle. More specifically, when inflation became rampant in 1979 and 1980, the Economic Recovery Tax Act of 1981 sharply shortened tax depreciation lives to offset inflation. Since then, inflation has fallen and depreciation lives for industrial and commercial struc-

Table 2. *Tax Rates at Which Housing Costs Are Deductible, by Income Class*[a]

Adjusted gross income (dollars)	Average tax rate		Marginal tax rate	
	Old law	New law	Old law	New law
13,000–25,000	14.6	07.4	16.6	17.6
25,000–30,000	21.1	12.8	18.9	18.0
30,000–50,000	27.9	24.2	25.1	18.4
50,000–100,000	40.2	31.6	36.4	31.6
100,000–200,000	47.1	37.0	45.5	37.0

a. Authors' calculations are based on the following assumptions: married couples with two dependents, one wage earner, the average fringe benefits and nonhousing itemized deductions of their income classes (based on 1983 Statistics of Income data), own houses of dollar value equal to twice their adjusted gross incomes, and pay property taxes equal to 1.2 percent of their house values. The methodology for computing these tax rates is discussed in Patric H. Hendershott and Joel Slemrod, "Taxes and the User Cost of Capital for Owner-Occupied Housing," *Journal of the American Real Estate and Urban Economics Association*, vol. 10 (Winter 1983), pp. 375–93.

tures have been lengthened (from 15 to 19 years). The 1986 act continues this lengthening.

Under previous law, residential rental property could be depreciated over 19 years using a 175 percent declining balance method with a switch to straight line in about the ninth year. Nonresidential property could use either straight line or the 175 percent declining balance method, but given the severity of the recapture provisions for those who used the accelerated procedure, most nonresidential property was depreciated using straight line. Equipment was depreciated over 5 years, on average, and public utility structures over 10 or 15 years; 150 percent declining balance with a switch to straight line was applicable to both asset types.

Under the new law, residential rental property is depreciable over 27.5 years and nonresidential property over 31.5 years. The depreciation method is straight line, and the recapture provisions are eliminated. Tax lives for public utility structures are lengthened to 15 or 20 years (still 150 percent declining balance). While tax lives of equipment are lengthened, a more accelerated method (200 percent declining balance versus the old 150 percent) is available. The net result is roughly no change in the present value of tax depreciation allowances. Finally, construction period interest and property tax (CPIT) expenses are added to the basis of the property; consequently, they will be amortized over either 27.5 or 31.5 years, compared with 10 years under previous law.

Tax Credits

Under the old law, tax credits existed for equipment, public utility structures, and rehabilitation expenditures on qualified properties, including historic structures and old or quasi-old nonresidential structures. The credits were 10 percent for equipment and public utility structures, 15 percent for quasi-old rehabilitation outlays, 20 percent for old rehabilitations, and 25 percent for historic structures. The depreciation basis was reduced by the full credit for the nonresidential rehabilitations and by half the credit for equipment and public utility and historic structures.

The new bill removes the credits for equipment, public utility structures, and rehabilitation of buildings built after 1936. For historic structures, the credit is cut from 25 to 20 percent, and the depreciable basis must now be reduced by the full credit. For old qualifying properties, the credit is lowered from 20 to 10 percent.[2] Our calculations suggest that assets that partially or totally lose their tax credits are the investment activities most disadvantaged by the tax reform act.

Interest Rates

The Tax Reform Act of 1986 has direct, negative implications for every type of capital good. Longer depreciation lives raise the investment hurdle rates (annual rental costs) for all structures except owner-occupied housing, and the reduction or elimination of investment tax credits increases hurdle rates for equipment, public utility structures, and rehabilitation projects. Finally, the cut in personal tax rates lowers the demand for depreciable real estate and owner-occupied housing. With the demand for all investment goods falling, interest rates will certainly decline. The magnitude of the decline depends on the interest sensitivities of both the supply of domestic and foreign saving and of investment demand itself. Hendershott has constructed a model in which total saving is independent of interest rates and the elasticity of the demands for capital is approximately unitary with respect to the rental prices of capital goods.[3] In this model, interest rates have to decline by 1.4 percentage points to offset the negative capital provisions of the act. That is, rates have to decline by this much to maintain *aggregate* investment at its previous level. A similar calculation with the more detailed Galper-Lucke-Toder model yields a 1.74 percentage point decline.[4]

2. These credits are subject to the same passive loss treatment as the credit for low-income rental housing (see below).

3. Patric H. Hendershott, "Tax Changes and Capital Allocation in the 1980s," in Martin Feldstein, ed., *The Effects of Taxation on Capital Formation* (University of Chicago Press, 1987).

4. Harvey Galper, Robert Lucke, and Eric Toder, "The Economic Effects of the Tax Reform Act of 1986," paper prepared for a Brookings Tax Conference, October 30–31, 1986.

Of course, interest rates will decline less if the supply of saving is reduced, and a reduction might be expected. On the domestic side, the deductibility of contributions to individual retirement accounts has been limited. IRA contributions for those with established pensions will no longer be deductible for households with incomes above $35,000 (singles) or $50,000 (married couples). Also, the maximum deductible annual contribution to supplemental retirement accounts has been lowered from $30,000 to $7,000. On the foreign side, any reduction in U.S. interest rates reduces returns to foreigners because they pay taxes based on foreign tax schedules, not U.S. schedules, and thus do not benefit from lower U.S. tax rates. However, international capital flows are not infinitely elastic, and even if they were, the United States is sufficiently large that its reduced investment demand would lower the world level of interest rates.

In the calculations reported below, we presume a 1 percentage point decline in U.S. interest rates. This does not mean that interest rates should be expected to decline by 100 basis points from the levels that existed on the act's enactment date; some of the rate decline probably occurred earlier in 1986.[5] All tax reform plans considered in 1986 proposed elimination of the investment tax credit for equipment and public utility structures retroactive to the beginning of 1986, and the likelihood that some version of tax reform would pass was high virtually all year. Thus the decline in interest rates and the weakness in equipment expenditures experienced in 1986 were partially attributable to the anticipated removal of this provision. Indeed, in the Hendershott model 75 of the 140 basis-point decline in interest rates is due solely to the elimination of this credit. Real estate probably benefited during much of 1986 from lower interest rates induced by tax reform.

Limits on tax shelters   The tax reform act contains multiple attacks on tax shelter activities: (1) the establishment of a new income category—passive income—from which losses are generally not deductible against other income, (2) a tightening of the limitations on interest expenses, (3) application (with major exceptions) of the at-risk rules to real estate, and (4) an expansion of the individual minimum tax.

5. The term "basis points" is often used instead of "percentage points" (100 basis points = 1 percentage point).

Passive Loss Limitations

For many years, different sources of income have been taxed differently under the federal tax code. For example, until 1981 "unearned" (nonlabor) income was subject to a far higher maximum tax rate than was "earned" or labor income. Capital gains have also generally been taxed less heavily than other income, owing to both the gains exclusion and deferral until realization. Moreover, portfolio capital losses, while fully deductible against portfolio capital gains, have been deductible against only $3,000 of other income.

The 1986 act introduces a new income class, passive income, and puts restrictions on passive losses somewhat analogous to those on portfolio capital losses. Passive income is defined to include income generated from business and trade activities in which the taxpayer does not materially participate *and* from rental activities such as real estate. For individuals, partnerships, trusts, and personal service corporations, losses from passive activities can be used to offset income from other passive activities, but not other income (such as wages and interest). Losses that cannot be claimed in a particular year can be "banked" and used to offset passive income in future years. Also, cumulative losses are allowed in full at the time of sale of the property if a gain or loss is recognized. The effective date for this provision is January 1, 1987, but a transition period was established for properties purchased before the law was signed by the president. The transition rule allows 65 percent of passive losses to be used to offset nonpassive income in 1987, 40 percent in 1988, 20 percent in 1989, and 10 percent in 1990.

An important exception applies to "small landlords." Taxpayers who actively manage residential rental investments may deduct up to $25,000 in losses against nonpassive income if their adjusted gross income computed without regard to the losses is less than $100,000. This amount is phased out at one dollar for every two dollars of income for taxpayers with incomes above $100,000, so that no losses are allowed for anyone who earns above $150,000. An identical exemption applies to tax credits in a deduction-equivalent sense; that is, $7,000 in credits is allowed because a $7,000 credit is equivalent to a $25,000 deduction for a taxpayer with a 28 percent tax rate. Active management requires that a taxpayer have at least a 10 percent interest in the property (and not be a limited partner) and be involved in the management of the property on a "substantial and continual" basis.

Two related rationales for the small landlord provision can be provided. The first is based upon uncertainty regarding the true nature of the income from actively managed properties. With active management, some of the income is earned income and thus should be treated like other earned income. The second rationale reflects the difficulties of real estate diversification for small investors attempting to use their management and maintenance skills. Diversification (by geographic area and real estate type) becomes particularly important when passive losses are deductible against only passive gains. Without diversification, large losses can more easily occur. While equity mutual funds allow small equity investors to diversify easily, real estate diversification for small managers or maintainers is impossible.

Other potentially important exceptions apply to certain types of corporations. Regular corporations are not subject to the rule, so they will be able to use passive losses to offset both regular and portfolio income of the corporation. Closely held corporations—other than personal service corporations that are subject to the at-risk rules (generally where five or fewer individuals own more than 50 percent of the stock)—can use passive losses to offset earned income, but not portfolio income (unearned income other than passive income).

Interest Expense Limitations

Previous law employed the concept of net investment income (investment income less investment expense) and investment interest expense (interest expense associated with investment income) to limit the amount of investment interest expense a taxpayer could deduct. The limit equaled $10,000 plus the amount of the taxpayer's net investment income. The new law will tighten the limitation by restricting the amount of investment interest expense that can be deducted to net investment income. Excess interest expense can be banked for possible deduction in future years, and the four-year transition period for passive losses applies.

In general, interest expense and income or losses for passive activities will not be included in the calculation of investment income or investment interest expense; that is, real estate is not subject to the interest expense limitation. However, during the transition period allowable passive losses (for example, 65 percent in 1987) will be subtracted from investment income. Thus a taxpayer for whom the investment interest expense limitation is binding will not obtain any relief from the transition rule for passive losses.

The new law prohibits the deduction of nonbusiness household interest except that on debt secured by first and second residences. Moreover, this interest is limited to that on mortgage debt that does not exceed the sum of the original purchase price of the properties, the cost of improvements, and educational and medical expenses that are incurred up to the current market value of the properties. The mortgage debt ceiling applies only to debt incurred after August 15, 1986. The prohibitions on nonmortgage, non-business household interest deductions are subject to the four-year transition period for passive losses.

At-Risk Rules

At-risk rules limit the cumulated deductible losses on an investment to the amount at risk (initial equity contribution plus cumulated taxable income less cumulated cash distributions plus recourse debt). To the extent that cumulative losses exceed investment at risk, the losses can be banked for future possible deductibility. Under old law, real estate was exempt from the at-risk rule.

The tax act extends the at-risk rules to real estate but simultaneously expands the definition of the amount at risk for real property to include nonrecourse debt secured by the property, including debt supplied on commercially reasonable terms by a lender with an equity interest in the property. Seller or installment sale financing, however, is not treated as nonrecourse debt. While this extension will obviously discourage seller financing, no general impact on the real estate market seems likely.

The Individual Minimum Tax

Individuals must pay the higher of their regular tax liability or their minimum tax liability. The latter is 21 percent of their income base—regular taxable income plus specified tax preferences less a $40,000 exemption for married taxpayers ($30,000 for singles or individual filers). The exemption is reduced 25 cents for each dollar by which the income base exceeds $150,000; during this phaseout, the effective tax rate is 26.5 percent.[6]

The 1986 act expands the list of tax preferences to include accelerated depreciation on equipment (the difference between 200

6. For a detailed discussion of both the individual and corporate minimum taxes, see Michael J. Graetz and Emil Sunley, "Minimum Taxes and Comprehensive Tax Reform," paper prepared for a Brookings Tax Conference, October 30–31, 1986.

percent declining balance and 150 percent declining balance), tax-exempt interest on new private activity bonds (those issued after August 7, 1986), and the appreciation component of charitable contributions. These expansions will increase the likelihood of taxpayers paying the minimum tax. However, the real estate tax preferences are reduced because accelerated depreciation and excluded capital gains on real estate no longer exist. Still remaining is the excess of tax depreciation over forty-year straight line. This could reduce the value of tax depreciation allowances by one-sixth.[7] Also, the reduction in taxable income resulting from an installment sale is a tax preference item. Moreover, during the transition period allowable passive losses will be included in the minimum tax.

Effects of Antishelter Provisions

Of all the antishelter provisions, only the new passive loss rules could plausibly affect real estate markets significantly. Four areas of possible impact include market rents, the volume of transactions, the form of financing, and the form of ownership.

Using the simulation methodology described below, we computed the worst-case effect of passive loss rules on rents under conditions of certainty. That is, the investment earns the expected return with certainty, and no passive gains on other investments are available to offset passive losses. Our analysis implies little effect. The combination of lengthened tax depreciation and CPIT deductions, lower interest rates, and higher rents virtually eliminates initial tax losses. Moreover, if passive losses were expected to be greater, as they would be in an environment of higher inflation (and thus higher interest rates), the financing would be restructured. The simplest method would be greater use of equity. Alternatively, debt with equity-kickers (share of asset appreciation or increase in rents) could be used to lower direct interest costs and thus passive losses.

The passive loss rules could still affect market rents, however. While no losses occur when the project "works," significant uncertainty surrounds the net operating income from properties, and losses would occur if this income falls significantly below expectations. If incomes from other projects are not sufficient to offset the passive losses, net losses would not be currently

---

7. The ratio of tax depreciation on a dollar of depreciable investment when the minimum tax is fully applied to tax depreciation with no minimum tax is $[\tau(1/27.5) - \tau_{min}(1/27.5 - 1/40)]/\tau(1/27.5)$, where τ is the regular tax rate and τ_{min} is the minimum rate. With $\tau = 0.52$ and $\tau_{min} = 0.257$ (0.21 plus the state and local tax), this ratio is 0.846.

deductible. This possibility would cause investors to raise the required expected return on real estate investments. Also acting to raise the required return is the reduction in importance of the relatively certain tax depreciation component of real estate investment vis-à-vis the relatively uncertain operating income and cash reversion component.

The passive loss rules will probably increase the number of real estate transactions. At any given time, some projects are likely to be souring—earning significant passive losses and promising to do so for some future periods—and others to be sweetening—earning above-expected returns and thus promising significant passive gains in the future. A sale of the sour project to the owner of the sweet one would allow the banked passive losses to be immediately deducted and would transfer the expected future losses to an owner who could use them as they accrue. While the sale price will be a distressed one, the buyer and seller will gain vis-à-vis the U.S. Treasury in that they will deduct the losses sooner.

A final issue is the impact on ownership form. Will large corporations increase their ownership of real estate because they are able to deduct passive losses against nonpassive income while individuals and partnerships are not? This seems likely in the short run when substantial passive losses on numerous projects exist, owing to both the large losses built into deals in the last few years and the high vacancy rates for many types of real estate in many areas of the country. In the longer run, however, expanded corporate ownership seems unlikely. For the first time in decades, the corporate income tax rate will be higher than the maximum personal tax rate. Moreover, the taxation of corporate income at the personal level may even be rising with the increase in the capital gains tax rate. The tax reform act is unlikely to be a boon to the corporate ownership form.

Effects on income-producing properties

In discussing the likely effects of the tax act upon the rents and values for rental and commercial real estate, we make a stylized distinction between the long- and short-run effects of the act. The short-run effect is to alter the values of existing properties, while the long-run effect is to alter the level of rents.

The pertinent real estate provisions are: the lengthening of tax depreciation from 19 years with 175 percent declining balance to 27.5 (or 31.5) years straight line, an extension of the deduction period for CPIT from 10 to 27.5 (or 31.5) years, the removal of the capital gains exclusion, and the cut in personal tax rates. All of these changes tend to raise rents and lower real estate values.

The precise tax rate change depends on the assumed marginal investor. For the new law, a marginal federal rate of 33 percent, which would be paid on taxable income of $72,000 to $193,000 (itemizing married couple with two dependents), seems reasonable enough. But the corresponding tax rates under the old law (indexed to 1988) range from 42 percent (on income of $68,000 to $97,000) to 49 percent (on $124,000 to $184,000), with 45 percent in between. Because of our uncertainty regarding the marginal investor, two sets of results will be reported, one starting with a 52 percent tax rate [0.49 + (1 − 0.49)0.06, where 0.06 is the presumed state and local income tax rate] and the other with a 45 percent rate [0.42 + (1 − 0.42)0.052]. In both cases, the marginal investor under new law is assumed to be in the 36 percent bracket [0.33 + (1 − 0.33)0.045, the lower state and local rate reflecting a presumed cut to offset the broadening of the tax base]. That is, the marginal rate will be cut by 16 and 9 percentage points, respectively.

The major assumptions underlying the analysis are an expected inflation rate of 4.5 percent, a risk-free interest rate of 9 percent applied to debt maintained at two-thirds of the market value of the project,[8] depreciation rates of 2½ percent in rents and 3 percent in structure price,[9] and a required after-tax return on equity of about 10.5 percent for the 52 percent tax bracket investor and 11.5 percent for the 45 percent investor.[10]

---

8. See Patric H. Hendershott and David C. Ling, "Likely Impacts of the Administration Proposal and H.R. 3838," in James R. Follain, ed., *Tax Reform and Real Estate* (Washington, D.C.: Urban Institute, 1986), pp. 87–112.

9. A potential problem with discounted cash flow models of this type is consistency between the assumed patterns of future rents and prices. See David C. Ling and Michael Whinihan, "Valuing Depreciable Real Estate: A New Methodology," *Journal of the American Real Estate and Urban Economics Association,* vol. 13 (Summer 1985), pp. 181–94. Assuming that rents are initially at the equilibrium level, the 2½ and 3 percent assumed depreciation rates provide consistency, that is, the resale price at year 20 is within 1 percent of the present value of cash flows beyond year 20. This consistency holds for both old law and the new tax act.

10. We compute the required equity rate, e, as:

$$e = (1 - t^*) \left[i + \frac{\beta}{1 - v} (rm - i) \right],$$

where t^* is a weighted average of the taxpayer's income and effective capital gains tax rates, i is the interest rate, β is the measure of the covariance of an unlevered real estate investment with the market return (assumed to be 0.5), v is the loan-to-value ratio, and $rm - i$ is the excess of the return on the market portfolio over the (risk-free) interest rate (assumed to be 0.06). The weights attached to the regular and effective capital gains tax

Effect on Equilibrium Rent Levels

The computational procedures employed to determine the change in equilibrium rent use a discounted cash flow model of an investment in real estate. The model takes into account the down payment, the expected after-tax cash flows, and the expected net reversion at sale. The long-run equilibrium level of rent is the initial rent that would equate the net present value of the investment to zero for a given set of assumptions (including inflation, interest rate, and required return on equity) and a particular tax regime. This rent per dollar of investment serves as a hurdle rate for prospective investors in income-producing properties. If a property can earn a rent greater than the equilibrium rent, then new units will be built to expand the supply of real estate. This process continues until the market rent declines to the equilibrium rent. On the other hand, if the equilibrium rent were to jump above the market rent, then new construction would be cut back until market rent rose to the new equilibrium value. The impact of the tax act upon rents is obtained by comparing the equilibrium level of rent under previous law to that required under the new law. In this computation, real estate value is assumed to equal its presumably unchanged replacement cost.

The equilibrium level of rent under the act must increase to replace the reduced tax benefits. Only then will investors in real estate earn a rate of return comparable to that on other investments of similar risk. Table 3 presents estimates of the likely rent increase for residential and commercial properties under alternative assumptions regarding the tax rate of the marginal investor in real estate and the size of the interest rate decline.

The top row indicates the equilibrium increase in rent assuming no change in interest rates for two different assumptions regarding the tax rate of the marginal investor under pre-1986 law. With a 45 percent marginal tax rate, residential rents will increase by 19 percent; with a 52 percent marginal rate, the rent increase is 33 percent. These increases are partially a result of increases in the required rate of return (81 and 182 basis points, respectively, for the 45 and 52 percent tax-bracket investors) owing to the generally lighter taxation of pretax returns on alternative investments.

---

rates, respectively, are ¾ and ¼. The capital gains tax rate is $(1-ex)\tau/2$, where *ex* is the long-term capital gains exclusion, τ is the regular income tax rate, and the division by 2 reflects deferral. For pre-1987 law, $\tau^* = 0.8\tau$; for the new law, $\tau^* = 0.875\tau$.

Table 3. *Increase in the Equilibrium Rent Level,*
under Various Assumptions
Percent

| | Marginal tax rate under old law | | | |
| | 45 percent | | 52 percent | |
Interest rate assumption	Residential	Commercial	Residential	Commercial
No decline	19	14	33	18
100 basis-point decline	11	6	24	10

Because ample evidence exists that taxpayers with tax rates far below the maximum are active in the rental market, the 19 percent increase seems more plausible than the 33 percent increase.

In the second row a 100 basis-point decline in interest rates (and a 68 basis-point decline in the required *after-tax* equity rate relative to that incorporated in the first row) is factored into the analysis. The result is a substantial reduction in the required residential rent increase: from 19 percent to 11 percent for the 45 percent tax-rate investor and from 33 percent to 24 percent for the 52 percent investor. (The rationale for believing that the tax act would lower interest rates was developed earlier.)

The required return on equity in real estate could rise relative to that on other investments because the importance of the relatively certain tax depreciation component of the return to real estate will decline vis-à-vis the less certain net operating income component. Moreover, real estate losses will no longer be deductible against nonpassive income. If one's passive activities should fall on hard times, the lack of deductibility against other income would result in the investor's shouldering the entire loss, as opposed to sharing it with the U.S. Treasury. A 1 percent increase in the required return would raise all equilibrium rent increases shown in table 3 by about 4 percentage points.

Our own view is that a 10 to 15 percent rent increase for residential properties is most likely. That is, we believe (1) the marginal investor under the old law to have been in the 45 percent tax bracket, (2) the likely decline in interest rates to be 100 basis points, and (3) some increase in the required return to be necessary to offset the increased riskiness of real estate investments.

The rent increases for commercial properties are lower. For the 45 percent tax rate, the percentage increases are about 5 points less; for the 52 percent tax rate, the increases are 15 points less. While tax depreciation for commercial properties is less generous than for residential under the new law, depreciation for the former was even less generous than for the latter under the old law. For commercial properties, then, the expected range of "rent" increases is 5 to 10 percent.

It is important to reiterate the process by which rents increase in competitive markets. Builders will find it less profitable to invest at the current level of rents with the new tax incentives than with the old ones. The combination of reduced new construction with normal growth in demand and steady obsolescence of the existing stock will eventually generate higher rents for the existing stock.

How quickly will rents rise from the old equilibrium level to the new? The rise will occur at the most rapid rate in fast-growing markets, and, the smaller the change in the equilibrium level, the sooner they will get to the new equilibrium. Of course, in markets with high vacancy rates this rise will occur only after current rents and occupancy rates get back to their equilibrium level under old law. Our best guess is that it will take four to twelve years for rents to rise to their new equilibrium level—the shorter time in cities like Columbus and the longer for commercial properties in cities like Houston.

Which provisions of the act are most responsible for the rent increases? Estimates of the effects of the individual provisions, including a change in the marginal tax rate from 45 to 36 percent, were computed two ways: the change in the equilibrium rent if a specific provision is the only change being made and the change when this provision is added after all other provisions—including a 100 basis-point decline in the interest rate—have been taken into account. Either way, the depreciation change increases rents about twice as much as the cut in the regular income tax rate does, and the effects of the CPIT deductions and capital gains exclusion are negligible. Removal of the capital gains exclusion is of little importance because (1) few gains are expected in a low-inflation environment, (2) gains are expected to be realized in the far distant future (see below), and (3) the gains exclusion is also removed on alternative investments, a fact that will lower the required return on real estate and thus tend to offset the direct impact of the exclusion removal.

Trading should decrease under the new law. Under old law, trading before tax depreciation disappeared in the nineteenth year was advantageous. Trading should not be optimal before the new tax depreciation life because a penalty to trading—the capital gains tax rate—has been increased and an advantage to trading—getting on the new depreciation schedule—has been decreased.[11] Moreover, the value of installment sale transactions, a method of dampening the capital gains tax penalty, is greatly reduced for sales of assets worth over $150,000 for sellers with substantial debt. In effect, the fraction of taxes that could formerly be deferred is reduced by the ratio of the seller's debt to the book value of assets.

Effect on the Value of Existing Properties

In considering the short-run impact of the act upon the value of existing real estate, we initially take the perspective of an investor in early 1987 contemplating the purchase of property put in place in 1986. This new investor will face a less generous tax depreciation schedule, a higher capital gains tax rate, a lower marginal tax rate, and, possibly, passive loss limitations. The question, then, is how much will this new investor alter his bid for the property relative to his bid under previous law? The standard of comparison is the price of the property that would have made it a zero net present value investment under the old law, assuming that rents were at their equilibrium level.

If rent instantaneously jumped to its new equilibrium level, then value would not decline; the higher rent would compensate exactly for the less generous tax rules. Because rent will not rise instantaneously, value will decline, the magnitude depending on how slowly investors *think* rent will rise to the new equilibrium level.[12] The longer the expected adjustment (the greater the present value of expected below-equilibrium rents), the greater the fall in value. A useful analogy can be drawn in the pricing of discount bonds. Bonds sell at a discount when they are earning a below-market coupon (rent). The more the coupon is below market and the longer the bonds are expected to earn the below-market coupon (the longer the bond's maturity), the lower is the market value relative to par.

Investor expectations of the rental adjustment process should vary with both the growth rate of the area and the extent of initial disequilibrium. We consider two growth rates (zero and positive) and three prereform states of the market (equilibrium, 10 percent

---

11. On optimal trading, see Patric H. Hendershott and David C. Ling, "Trading and the Tax Shelter Value of Depreciable Real Estate," *National Tax Journal,* vol. 37 (June 1984), pp. 213–23.

12. See Patric H. Hendershott and David C. Ling, "Prospective Changes in Tax Law and the Value of Depreciable Real Estate," *Journal of the American Real Estate and Urban Economics Association,* vol. 12 (Fall 1984), pp. 297–317.

"excess capacity," and 20 percent excess capacity). In all cases, depreciation or obsolescence is assumed to occur at the rate of 2 percent per year. Thus 10 percent of excess capacity or below-market rents would be eliminated in five years even with zero growth. The positive growth market is assumed to eliminate 5 percent excess capacity per year, 2 percent for obsolescence and 3 percent for growth. Thus 30 percent of below-market rents (20 percent due to excess capacity and 10 percent due to tax reform) would be eliminated in six years in the high-growth area and in fifteen years in the no-growth area.

The upper half of table 4 contains estimates of the percentage declines in value of a property purchased in early 1987 caused by an 11 percent increase in equilibrium rents and the failure of actual rents to increase immediately to that level. The first row is for a property that would have had a zero net present value under the old law, that is, was in equilibrium before the enactment of the tax act. As can be seen, the decline in value is a modest 1 percent in a growth market and 2 percent in a no-growth market.

Rows 2 and 3 pertain to cases of 10 and 20 percent excess capacity. In these calculations, we first compute the total percentage price discount from reproduction cost and then attribute some of it to the initial disequilibrium and the remainder to tax reform. The value declines are far larger when substantial excess capacity exists. The tax act reduces value from an already depressed level by 7 or 8 percent in no-growth areas, compared with only

Table 4. *Estimates of Property Value Changes*[a]
Percent

Purchase date and market or tax status	Fast growth		No growth	
	Total price discount	Discount due to reform	Total price discount	Discount due to reform
Purchased January 1, 1987				
1. In equilibrium	−1	−1	−2	−2
2. 10 percent excess capacity	−5	−4	−9	−7
3. 20 percent excess capacity	−9	−4	−16	−8
Held by investor after purchase date				
4. December 1, 1986, no passive loss limits	. . .	5.3	. . .	5.2
5. December 1, 1986, passive loss limits fully binding	. . .	−2.2	. . .	−2.6
6. October 1, 1986, passive loss limits fully binding but transition rules applicable	. . .	−0.5	. . .	−1.4

a. Assuming an 11 percent increase in equilibrium rents.

4 percent in a growth area. The 8 percent decline is probably the upper bound. The assumption of an 11 percent rent increase and 20 percent excess capacity is a worst-case commercial scenario and is probably equivalent to a worst-case rental scenario. While greater increases are possible for rental properties, excess capacity is far less.

The perspective taken above was that of a new buyer of the property in early 1987; an alternative perspective is that of the current owner of a new property placed in service in 1986. The value of the investment to this person will exceed the value to the 1987 purchaser because this person will be able to use the more generous tax depreciation schedule from previous law and, if he purchased before October 22, 1986, the passive loss transition rules. The computations are contained in the lower half of table 4. The value to this investor rises even if rents are expected to take five years to adjust (the no-growth assumption), so long as the passive loss limits are not binding. That is, the present value of the tax saving from the more favorable tax depreciation exceeds the present value of the below-market rents. However, if the investor has no passive income to offset passive losses and is not eligible for the transition rules (row 5), the more generous depreciation is of no value. Because this investor is worse off than the marginal investor, who we assume is not affected by the passive loss limits, value declines are greater than those shown in row 1. Finally, if this investor purchased the property before October 22, 1986 (row 6), the decline in value would be less than that of the marginal investor who purchased in 1987. That is, the transition rules would almost allow the investor to maintain value.

A comparison of row 1 with rows 4–6 yields interesting implications about trading in 1987. Row 1 can be viewed as the maximum bid price, relative to reproduction cost, of an investor for a property in 1987, whereas rows 4–6 give the relative value to property owners in different tax situations. An owner will sell only if the bid price of a new investor exceeds the value of holding the property. These numbers suggest (1) a strong disincentive by owners not subject to the passive loss limits to trade properties purchased in 1986, (2) a mild disincentive for owners subject to the limits but eligible for the transition rules, and (3) a strong incentive to trade by those subject to the limits and not eligible for the transition rules. In fact, in our model the latter investors trade in the first or second period to maximize their return (minimize their loss). A disincentive to trade also holds for investors not subject to the loss limits who purchased properties in earlier years, but the disincentive is less the earlier the property was purchased, because of the more generous depreciation allowances under the old law.

Effect on owner-occupied housing

Current law grants important benefits to homeowners: imputed rental income is not taxed, and capital gains are rarely taxed and then only on a much-deferred basis. Moreover, the deductibility of home mortgage interest ensures that itemizing households with mortgages will benefit fully from the nontaxation of owner-occupied housing. A consequence of these favorable provisions is that homeowners receive substantial tax subsidies. The higher the marginal tax rate of an individual, the larger the subsidy and the lower the after-tax cost of owner-occupied housing.

The 1986 tax act does not directly alter any of these favorable provisions, but it does affect the after-tax cost of owner-occupied housing. First, the tax rates at which households deduct housing costs are reduced. Second, the pretax level of interest rates will be lower. Furthermore, the combination of changes in owner costs and market rents will probably change the aggregate homeownership rate.

The annual after-tax cost of obtaining one dollar of housing capital depends upon the cost of debt, the cost of contributed equity, property taxes, real economic depreciation, expected appreciation, and the tax savings associated with owner-occupied housing. Two costs or "prices" of owner housing are relevant: the average cost, which influences the tenure choice decision; and the marginal cost, which affects the quantity demanded by households that choose to own. The average and marginal costs vary inversely with the average and marginal tax rates at which housing costs are deductible.

Estimates of owner housing costs per hundred dollars of housing capital for households in different income classes under both the old law and the new tax act are contained in table 5, based on the tax rates listed in table 1.[13] If interest rates are not affected by the tax act, then the *marginal* cost will be unchanged for households with incomes under $30,000 but will rise by roughly 10 percent for those with higher incomes because of the general decrease in the tax rates at which marginal housing costs are deducted. If, however, interest rates decline by 1 percentage point, as we expect, then households with incomes below about $30,000 will experience

13. For details on the precise methodology underlying these calculations, see Hendershott and Ling, "Likely Impacts of the Administration Proposal and H.R. 3838."

Table 5. *Marginal and Average After-Tax Cost per $100 of Owner-Occupied Housing, by Income Class*
Dollars

Adjusted gross income (dollars)	Old law		New law			
			9 percent interest rate		8 percent interest rate	
	Marginal	Average	Marginal	Average	Marginal	Average
13,000–25,000	8.18	8.51	8.08	9.09	7.29	8.20
25,000–30,000	7.95	7.77	8.04	8.65	7.26	7.72
30,000–50,000	7.34	7.00	8.00	7.43	7.22	6.73
50,000–100,000	6.33	6.10	6.70	6.70	6.24	6.24
100,000–200,000	5.67	5.50	6.29	6.29	5.88	5.88

about a 10 percent decrease in marginal housing costs, households with incomes above about $130,000 will face a 5 percent increase, and the change for other households will be negligible. Thus any tendency toward softer house prices will be confined to only the very high end of the market (over $250,000) and will be modest in magnitude.

Without a decline in interest rates, *average* housing costs increase 5 to 10 percent across the board. They increase for households with incomes below $30,000, in spite of roughly no change in marginal tax rates, because the tax act both raises the standard deduction and reduces nonhousing-related itemized deductions (such as sales taxes and consumer interest), causing more housing deductions of these households to be wasted than was the case under the old law. With a 1 percentage point decline in interest rates, however, average housing costs will decrease slightly for households with incomes below approximately $60,000; households with incomes above about $120,000 will experience a 5 percent increase in costs.

Homeownership depends on, among other things, the ratio of the average cost of owning to the cost of renting. The percentage changes in these ratios for households in various income classes are reported in table 6. The calculations in the first column assume no decline in interest rates and no change in rents. The next two columns assume a 1 percentage point decline in interest rates, with no change in rents and with a 10 percent increase in rental costs. Because rents are held constant in the first two columns, the percentage changes equal the percentage changes in average owner costs for each income level. With the interest rate decline and no rent increase, homeownership is modestly more attractive for households with incomes below about $60,000 and slightly less attractive for higher-income households. With the rise in

Table 6. *Effect of the 1986 Tax Act on the Ratio of Average Owner Costs to Rental Costs, by Income Class*
Percent

Adjusted gross income (dollars)	Percentage change in ratio of costs		
	9 percent rate, no change in rents	8 percent rate, no change in rents	8 percent rate, 10 percent increase in rents
13,000–25,000	7	−4	−12
25,000–30,000	10	−1	−10
30,000–50,000	6	−4	−13
50,000–100,000	10	2	−7
100,000–200,000	14	7	−2

rents, all currently renting households will find homeownership more attractive than under the old law. Overall, the aggregate homeownership rate should eventually rise by about 3 percentage points.

Low-income rental housing

Tax incentives to stimulate the construction of low-income rental housing have been part of the law for many years. Previous law allowed investors in low-income properties to depreciate the properties over fifteen years and to use a 200 percent declining balance method; in addition, CPIT would be expensed during the construction period. Furthermore, investors often had access to tax-exempt financing at rates substantially below market.

The tax act changes this law in two important respects. First, the preferential depreciation and construction period write-off schedules are replaced with a system of tax credits that depends upon the type of housing purchased or built and whether the project has access to tax-exempt financing or other types of subsidy. Specifically, the investor receives:

1. An annual credit for ten years that has a present value equal to 70 percent of the cost of construction (both new and substantially rehabilitated projects) placed in service between January 1, 1987, and December 31, 1989. For 1987, the applicable Treasury discount rate converts into a 9 percent annual credit, but this credit will rise if interest rates rise and fall if rates decline.

2. For existing low-income housing or new construction with tax-exempt financing or other rental housing subsidies, the present value of the credit is 30 percent (the annual credit for 1987 is 4 percent).

The depreciable basis is not reduced by the credit. The second change is a reduction in the availability of tax-exempt financing.

An analogy to the passive loss limits applies to these credits, as does a "small landlord provision." The latter says that up to $7,000 in credits can be used to offset taxes on regular or portfolio income by households with taxable income below $200,000 (no active management criterion need be met). The offset is phased out between $200,000 and $250,000. With a 9 percent annual credit, an investment of up to $77,778 is eligible for the full offset.

Potentially severe restrictions are placed upon investments to qualify investors for the credits. First, at least 20 percent of the units must be occupied by tenants whose income cannot exceed 50 percent of the area's median income adjusted for family size, or 40 percent must be occupied by tenants with income under 60 percent of the area's median. Only the units so occupied receive the credit. (Previous law defined qualifying income as 80 percent of the area's median income.) Second, tenants cannot pay more than 30 percent of their income in rent. Third, the project must satisfy these criteria fifteen years after it is placed in service or purchased, or a substantial penalty will be levied. Fourth, the total value of the credits issued in a state is limited to $1.25 times the population of the state.

A number of difficult conceptual problems exist in modeling low-income housing. These include specifying the expected sales prices at year 15 and beyond and the depreciation rates and required equity returns, both presumably higher than their counterparts for regular rental housing. These and other problems must be addressed before a definitive statement can be made on the treatment of low-income housing in the tax act vis-à-vis old law. Nonetheless, we have made a few "minimum" rent calculations that are probably instructive.

The minimum rent required by investors to earn their required rate of return is half as large with the new 9 percent credit as it was under old law, even when tax-exempt financing was employed (the debt rate was 200 basis points below market). With the 4 percent credit and tax-exempt financing, the minimum rent is roughly the same as under old law with tax-exempt financing. This suggests two things. First, the 9 percent credit dominates the 4 percent credit with tax-exempt financing. Thus limits on tax-exempt financing for low-income housing may not be important. Second, the 9 percent credit is far more generous than under old law. Whether the credit is sufficient to generate a substantial increase in the construction of low-income housing is unknown, however.

Summary

In contrast to the conventional wisdom, the 1986 tax act does not discourage real estate activity in the aggregate. Within the broad real estate aggregate, however, widely different effects are to be expected. Regular rental and commercial activity will be slightly disfavored (modest increases in rents and declines in values will occur), and historic and old rehabilitation activity will be greatly disfavored. In contrast, owner-occupied housing, by far the largest component of real estate, is favored, both directly by an interest rate decline and indirectly by the increase in rents. Homeownership should rise significantly, and the quantity and value of houses should increase slightly, except at the very high end of the market. Low-income rental housing may be the most favored of all activities.

The rent increase for residential properties will be 10 to 15 percent with our assumption of a 1 percentage point decline in interest rates. For commercial properties, the expected rent increase is 5 to 10 percent. The market value decline will be greater the longer and farther investors think rents will be below the new equilibrium. It is unlikely to exceed 4 percent in fast-growth markets, even if substantial excess capacity currently exists. Moreover, the value of recently purchased properties to current holders not subject to the passive loss limits will generally rise, because the more generous tax depreciation allowances under old law add more value than the expected below-market rent subtracts. In no-growth markets with substantial excess capacity, market values could decline by as much as 8 percent from already depressed levels.

Two offsetting factors operate on the after-tax cost of owner-occupied housing. Lower tax rates increase the cost, but lower interest rates decrease it. With a 1 percentage point decline in interest rates, the after-tax marginal cost will fall by about 10 percent for most households with incomes below $30,000 and rise by about 5 percent for those with incomes above $130,000. Thus only the highest-priced houses would experience weakness in value. Average housing costs will decrease slightly in this scenario for households with incomes below about $60,000, but will increase by 5 percent for those with incomes above twice this level. With the projected increase in rents, homeownership should rise for all income classes, but especially for those with incomes under $60,000. The aggregate homeownership rate is projected to increase by 3 percentage points in the long run in response to the tax act.

The new passive loss limitations are likely to lower significantly the values of loss-motivated partnership deals and of properties in areas where vacancy rates have risen sharply. The limitations should have little impact on new construction and market rents, however. Reduced depreciation write-offs, lower interest rates, and higher rents all act to lower expected passive losses. Moreover, financing can be restructured to include equity-kickers or less debt generally at little loss of value.

Comments by Robert Gladstone

THE REAL ESTATE SECTOR was a key target of the tax reform act. Changes in ground rules for taxing real estate investments are perhaps among the most drastic of those in the act. In overall terms, virtually all key tax benefits and subsidies, for instance, have been eliminated for commercial real estate, although benefits of residential ownership have been substantially maintained. The effects will certainly be profound.

This paper by Patric Hendershott, James Follain, and David Ling confirms widely held beliefs about the law's effect on real estate investment. The paper also performs a valuable service in quantifying the dimensions of those effects and, in doing so, emphasizes interest rates as a dynamic ingredient. What the paper does not do is to establish whether the act's effects are healthy or unhealthy for the real estate industry and for the industry's effects on the economy.

Before going on to discuss certain conclusions reached by the authors, I would like to comment on these effects from the perspective of a real estate developer-owner. The real estate community is, of course, sharply divided on this subject.

Together with some of my colleagues in the industry, I believe past real estate tax preferences diverted too much capital into unproductive investments, contributing to the glut of development, particularly of office space, prevalent in so many markets throughout the United States. As a result, real costs and market inefficiencies increased significantly. The preferences subsidized rents, masked substandard returns on investment, and favored real estate at the expense of other sectors in the economy. They reduced apparent risk and distorted investment decisionmaking by offering predictable tax deductions, which have totaled two or four or even more times the initial equity commitments in certain real estate deals.

There may at one time have been public policy justifications for such preferences, but, with perhaps the exception of such socially based programs as low- and moderate-income housing, the justifications no longer exist. In short, the motivating philosophy of the new law is fair and appropriate. Neither the nation nor the industry was well served by the previous law.

Under that law the real estate industry became too big. Its capacity and compulsion to produce was and is too great in relation to the capacity or appetite of the market to absorb space. Population and job growth, even when taken together with replacement demand and obsolescence, have not expanded the market quickly enough.

To the extent that the new tax law encourages an orderly shrinkage of the real estate industry, I believe it will be a positive force. Shrinkage in output and in the number of producers can be accomplished perhaps uniquely well in the real estate industry because of its structure and relatively low level of capitalization in fixed assets compared with other major U.S. industries. It is conventional in the real estate industry to contend with volatile markets and rapid cyclical changes in output from year to year and over several years. Historically, for instance, housing starts have swung from 1 million units a year to 2 million and back again over relatively short periods. Commercial markets in metropolitan areas often expand by a factor of two, then shrink again in the course of several years. Yet the industry has been able to deal with these expansions and contractions reasonably well.

Having said that the new law will be a positive force in the real estate industry, I also believe that the period and process of transition are especially sensitive matters. Among other issues is the treatment of investments in real estate deals made in good faith under the old law. Is it fair to have changed the ground rules in the middle of the game? Because of the changes, many see the prospect of major business disruption and extensive litigation.

If Hendershott, Follain, and Ling present few conclusions about the effect of the new law on the real estate sector, they do examine closely the potential changes in the general economy in relation to the changes in preferential treatment of real estate investment. They conclude that rents for commercial and residential properties will increase even as values for these properties decline and stay depressed pending occurrence of the full rent increases projected.

But how descriptive of real world situations are inputs to the models and therefore the results forecast? For example, a case can be made for declines rather than increases in rents, even assuming, as the paper does, that interest rates will decline.

The case for declining rents rests on the highly elastic demand for rental real estate with respect to price. This results because demand for real estate is much more discretionary than usually supposed and, in addition, is increasingly footloose in its locational patterns.

At the same time, however, pressures to increase rents and prices are enormous. These pressures include higher land costs driven by scarcity brought on through local government regulations and fiscal controls, increases in the cost of labor and materials despite some production cutbacks, and escalations in operating costs caused by rising state and local taxes and utility rates. These pressures exist in addition to new pressures to increase yields as a result of changes in the tax law. In such a situation perhaps the only cost decrease would be for interest, as the authors point out.

In the marketplace, owners respond to increased costs by attempting to increase rents. But highly price-sensitive, discretionary demand then shrinks, making it difficult to sustain the increases. Contractions in production can also be expected because of inadequate returns, although such corrections will occur very slowly.

These conditions characterize many local real estate markets today, including those with vigorous growth patterns and moderate levels of new development. The question we must ask is whether the basic supply and demand factors, for which the model described by the authors does not fully account, are so powerful that they could overwhelm the predicted interest rate decreases and the tendency for rent increases.

A case can also be made for flat or increasing values for commercial properties, even in the short term, as opposed to the falling values forecast by the model. The case would go something like this: property buyers, acting on the conviction that rents will increase later and that interest rates will decrease—both as forecast—make calculations of present values justifying higher rather than lower prices. Specifically, the effects on the present value of expected rent increases and falling interest costs are projected to more than offset any tax benefits lost. This would be especially true for institutional buyers, such as pension funds, that are not sensitive to tax considerations.

The time to test this trend will be in 1987, when the year-end 1986 flurry of transactions will have subsided among sellers seeking to capture lower rates of tax on capital gains and buyers seeking shorter depreciation cycles.

The authors' calculations thus correctly illustrate important tendencies that can be expected to operate in the next few years. The calculations, however, do not and probably cannot deal with the full range of market complexities that are affected by the 1986 act.

But whatever its immediate economic effects, the new law should be beneficial in rationalizing the real estate industry by scaling back tax considerations as a factor in investment decision-making.

Comments by John Yinger

THIS PAPER by Patric Hendershott, James Follain, and David Ling provides a careful, detailed look at the impact of the Tax Reform Act of 1986 on real estate. The authors conclude that the act is likely to cause apartment rents to rise by 10 to 15 percent but have little effect on owner-occupied housing except in the highest income brackets, where homeownership costs will rise 5 percent. As a result, the act is likely to cause some renters to buy homes. These results are similar to those obtained by Poterba and by researchers at the National Association of Home Builders using similar methodologies.[14]

To provide some perspective on this analysis, I evaluate the authors' methodology and use their results to determine whether the changes in the tax treatment of housing are good or bad.

Methodology   The authors' examination of the act is thorough. The only provision they neglect is one with minor but somewhat unusual effects, namely the unique ability of homeowners to deduct interest. Renters who need to borrow a large amount to start a business, say, or to send their children to college may be able to lower their interest expenses by 28 or 33 percent (depending on their tax bracket) by becoming homeowners. In addition, homeowners who purchased their houses a long time ago cannot deduct interest on a loan greater than the purchase price of their houses plus the cost of improvements and may also have an incentive to move. One can imagine two neighbors with identical houses who sell to each other—with no change in their house values—and thereby increase their interest deductions.

The methodology of the paper has been developed in a series

14. See James M. Poterba, "Tax Reform and Residential Investment Incentives," paper presented at the National Tax Association Annual Meeting, Washington, D.C., November 1986; and National Association of Home Builders, *Home Building after Tax Reform* (Washington, D.C.: NAHB, 1986).

of articles, many by the authors, over the past few years.[15] The methodology takes the perspective of an investor and simulates the long-run impact of tax reform on rents (actual for rental housing, implicit for owner-occupied housing). One key assumption is that investors must earn an equal return on all investments; that is, the long-run supply of funds to each investment alternative is perfectly elastic. This assumption allows the authors to determine how much rents must change to offset the act's impact on the return on investment in housing. Any required increase in rents is moderated by a decline in the rate of return on other assets caused by other provisions of the act. The authors assume, based on other studies, that the act will lower the overall rate of return in the economy by 1 percentage point.

The assumption that the supply of funds to housing is perfectly elastic is plausible but, to my knowledge, has never been tested. Some investors may be willing, for example, to accept a lower return on housing than on other assets either because of personal benefits from homeownership or satisfaction from providing housing to others. It is, of course, unfair to blame the authors for the fact that housing markets have not been adequately studied. Their methodology is clever precisely because it yields plausible results despite the complexity of the problem and the lack of evidence about some key factors. Nevertheless, it would also be unwise to accept as the last word a simulation based on untested assumptions.

A second problem with the methodology is that it depends on an oversimplified characterization of housing supply. The rent calculation is carried out for a single representative housing investment, not for a distribution of housing investments with different characteristics. The authors assume, in effect, that all housing is supplied by new construction. But in fact most housing is provided by existing buildings with widely varying maintenance, mortgage interest, depreciation, and other characteristics. Moreover, with sufficient maintenance, existing buildings can continue to provide housing indefinitely. Some analysts have argued, for example, that many housing projects are supplied at the current rent level because they involve large passive losses that can be offset against other income.[16] Thus the increase in rents needed to compensate investors for the provisions of the act

15. See James R. Follain, ed., *Tax Reform and Real Estate* (Washington, D.C.: Urban Institute, 1986) and references cited there.
16. See, for example, Anthony Downs, *Rental Housing in the 1980s* (Brookings, 1983).

may be greater for existing than for new housing. All housing requires an increase in rents because of less generous depreciation and lower marginal rates; some existing housing requires an additional increase in rents because the act diminishes the value of passive losses. An urban area in which new construction is not economical and in which many housing units involve large passive losses may therefore experience a larger increase in rents than the authors predict.[17]

Although the authors focus on long-run changes in rents, they also provide some intriguing but sketchy predictions about short-run changes in market values. The calculations in the paper yield the rent per dollar of investment that is needed for long-run equilibrium. This is not the same thing as the rent per apartment (or per unit of housing services).[18] Consider an existing apartment building. How can the rent per dollar of investment rise enough to offset the effects of the act? First, the rent on every apartment can go up with no change in total investment (that is, in the market price of the building). Second, the total investment can drop with no change in the rent per apartment. The second possibility, which involves capital losses for the owners of existing apartment buildings, immediately establishes short-run investor equilibrium. For new construction, the market price must equal construction cost, so the investment cannot drop. Until apartment rents rise, therefore, the act will greatly reduce or eliminate new construction in rental housing.

---

17. A large share of the rental housing in some cities consists of two- or three-family units with a resident owner. Because these owners often develop a long-term relationship with their tenants, their rent is often below market levels and their rental income for tax purposes is negative. The provision of the act that allows "active" landlords to use up to $25,000 of passive losses to offset other income may help to keep these landlords in business without large rent increases.

18. By definition the rent per unit of housing is the rent per dollar of investment multiplied by the investment needed to obtain a unit of housing. The supply curve for housing describes how the investment needed to obtain a unit of housing changes as the quantity of housing changes. The authors assume that the investment per unit of housing is constant (that is, the housing supply curve is horizontal) and is not affected by the act. These assumptions greatly simplify the problem because they ensure that the rent per unit of housing is determined entirely on the supply side; with a horizontal supply curve, the equilibrium rent is the same for every level of demand. This approach would be appropriate if all housing were provided by new construction; the prevailing view among economists is that new housing is produced with constant costs. As noted, however, most housing is supplied by existing buildings, and the cost of providing a unit of housing varies widely from one building to another. In other words, the housing supply curve is upward sloping, at least until new construction becomes economical. In a city without new construction, therefore, one cannot determine the equilibrium rent without considering the demand for housing—thereby vastly complicating the analysis.

The paper includes a section on these short-run capital losses. The authors point out that these losses will vary with the timing of the sale because some sales are subject to transition rules. They also calculate capital losses under various assumptions about rent increases anticipated by investors. These calculations are useful but leave one wanting more. What is the distribution of anticipated rent increases? How many buildings are subject to transition rules? The authors provide no data on these points and therefore reach no conclusions about the distribution of short-run losses.

Over time, of course, some apartments will be demolished or converted to condominiums or nonhousing uses: that is, the supply of housing will decrease and market rents will rise. How fast will this rise occur? The answer obviously depends on growth in housing demand and on the details of housing removals and conversions. The authors present some illustrative calculations but do not provide any data. One is left wondering whether the transition will take five years or twenty-five years in most cities.

Finally, changes in housing markets involve complex patterns of household moves—sometimes called filtering. Roughly speaking, the highest-income households move into new housing, and others move into housing vacated by households with incomes greater than theirs. These trades depend on the characteristics of existing housing and on the possibilities for renovation and conversion, which differ widely among metropolitan areas and are not considered in this paper. Such trades among households are a key determinant of changes in housing consumption and tenure and, in a city without new construction, of long-run rents. Furthermore, the trades influence important outcomes at the neighborhood level, such as the extent of housing abandonment or rehabilitation. The act's passive loss provisions, which favor small landlords, and its low-income housing credits, which have complex requirements (discussed below), may lead to different patterns of trades in different cities. I hope that future research, such as simulations with the Urban Institute's metropolitan housing model, addresses these issues.[19]

Evaluation of the new tax treatment of housing

The authors provide a detailed analysis of the act's housing provisions but do not evaluate them. As a guide for policymakers, I will draw on their results to lay out some of the key issues for such an evaluation.

19. See Alan Fox and others, "The Effects of Tax Reform on Metropolitan Housing," in James R. Follain, ed., *Tax Reform and Real Estate* (Washington, D.C.: Urban Institute, 1986), pp. 165–86.

Let us first examine the impacts of the new housing provisions on equity. One issue, the impact of the act on low-income renters, is particularly important. Several recent studies have found that low-income renters face declining housing quality and increasing rent burdens.[20] In 1983, for example, the median rent burden (rent plus utilities as a share of income) for renters in the bottom fifth of the income distribution was 46 percent. As several analysts have pointed out, low-income households have little to gain from lower marginal rates or a higher zero bracket amount because they pay little or no tax to begin with. These households do, however, have a lot to lose from higher rents because rents consume such a large share of their income.[21] Consequently, a 10 to 15 percent increase in rents poses a potentially serious problem of equity.

The act's new credit for the construction and rehabilitation of low-income housing may help alleviate this problem. The authors carry out a preliminary analysis and conclude the credit is very generous: people eligible for it may be able to provide low-income housing at lower-than-current rents. Qualifying for the credit may be difficult, however. A large share of the tenants must have low incomes, they cannot pay more than 30 percent of their income in rent, and the project must meet these restrictions for fifteen years. A careful analysis by Diamond concludes that, although regulations for qualifying are very complex, the credit may stimulate low-income housing production and rehabilitation under some circumstances.[22]

Because the federal government has virtually eliminated its direct subsidies of low-income housing, this tax credit may be the only tool available to offset the high rent burdens faced by the poor and the likely increase in these burdens because of the act. Federal policymakers may, however, be able to help alleviate the burdens by helping local governments and developers devise projects that meet the requirements of the act.

The new housing programs' other effects on equity are modest. One effect is progressive: the decline in the top marginal tax rate

20. See William C. Apgar, "Recent Trends in Housing Quality and Affordability: A Reassessment," MIT-Harvard Joint Center for Urban Studies, 1985; and H. James Brown and John Yinger, "Homeownership and Housing Affordability in the United States: 1974–85," MIT-Harvard Joint Center for Urban Studies, 1986.

21. See William C. Apgar and H. James Brown, "Assessment of the Likely Impacts of the President's Tax Proposals on Rental Housing Markets," MIT-Harvard Joint Center for Urban Studies, 1985; and Poterba, "Tax Reform and Residential Investment Incentives."

22. Douglas B. Diamond, Jr., "The Low-Income Rental Housing Credit," in National Association of Home Builders, *Home Building after Tax Reform*, pp. 57–72.

lowers the value of housing deductions to the richest homeowners, thereby raising their ownership costs slightly.[23] Other effects are somewhat regressive: moderate-income renters face increasing rents, whereas most owners, who typically have higher incomes, face no change in housing costs. This regressive impact may gradually be moderated as renters become homeowners.

The impacts of the new housing provisions on efficiency are more difficult to determine.[24] A tax law can distort households' choices between types of housing and between housing and other assets. Most analysts have argued that previous law provided favorable treatment for rental housing relative to other assets and even more favorable treatment for owner-occupied housing. One might conclude, therefore, that the new provisions enhance efficiency by eliminating many of the tax breaks for rental housing and by lowering the impact of the homeownership deductions through lower marginal tax rates.

This conclusion may not be correct, however, because it is based solely on the lessening of the distortion in household choices between housing and other assets. The relatively favorable treatment of housing has indeed been modified by the act, but the favorable treatment of owner-occupied housing relative to rental housing has been magnified. Decreased distortion at one margin may have been offset by increased distortion at another. Unfortunately, there is no consensus on the right way to tax owner-occupied housing, so one cannot be certain about the magnitude of the distortion at the renter–owner margin.[25] My own guess is that the increase in efficiency caused by lowering the value of tax breaks for housing relative to other assets was only partially offset by an increase in inefficiency caused by raising tax breaks for owner-occupied housing relative to rental housing.

23. Poterba finds a somewhat larger increase, 31 percent, in the cost of homeownership for the richest households; see "Tax Reform and Residential Investment Incentives."

24. The efficiency issues are reviewed by James R. Follain and Jan K. Brueckner, "Federal Income Taxation and Real Estate: Tax Distortions and Their Impacts," in Follain, ed., *Tax Reform and Real Estate*, pp. 9–26.

25. Several analysts have argued that owner-occupied housing involves positive externalities, so that up to some point tax breaks for homeownership enhance efficiency. In addition, the property tax may be a source of distortion in housing markets so that efficiency in the second-best sense requires some tax breaks for housing. Finally, I have argued elsewhere that the capitalization of public service levels into house values leads to underconsumption of housing in many communities. See "Inefficiency and the Median Voter: The Property Tax, Capitalization, Heterogeneity and the Theory of the Second Best," in J. M. Quigley, ed., *Perspectives on Local Public Finance and Public Policy*, vol. 2 (Greenwich, Conn.: JAI Press, 1985), pp. 3–30.

Conference Participants

with their affiliations at the time of the conference

Henry J. Aaron
Brookings Institution

Donald C. Alexander
Cadwalader, Wickensham & Taft

Andrea Andrews
Price Waterhouse

Emily S. Andrews
Employee Benefit Research Institute

Russel Baris
Pfizer Pharmaceuticals

Eileen Beall
Lockheed Missiles and Space Company

Edward M. Bernstein
Brookings Institution

David Berson
Wharton Econometrics

Paul Boltz
T. Rowe Price

Barbara A. Butler
Bell Atlantic

Mortimer Caplin
Caplin and Drysdale

John E. Chapoton
Vinson & Elkins

Sheldon S. Cohen
Morgan, Lewis & Bockius

Thomas Cunningham
Federal Reserve Bank of Atlanta

William G. Dakin
Mobil Corporation

103

Gina Despres
Office of Senator Bill Bradley

Bill Diefenderfer
Wunder, Thelen & Forgotson

Larry L. Dildine
Price Waterhouse

E. William Dinkelacker
Office of Management and Budget

Roscoe L. Egger, Jr.
Price Waterhouse

A. Lee Fritschler
Brookings Institution

Don Fullerton
Department of the Treasury

Harvey Galper
Brookings Institution

Bruce L. Gensemer
Kenyon College

Martin Ginsburg
Georgetown University Law Center

Robert Giordano
Goldman, Sachs and Company

Robert Gladstone
Quadrangle Development Corporation

Jane G. Gravelle
Congressional Research Service

John W. Gray, Jr.
American Telephone & Telegraph

George Guttman
Research Institute of America

Daniel Halperin
Georgetown University Law Center

David E. Harrington
Kenyon College

Patric H. Hendershott
Ohio State University

Charles R. Hulten
University of Maryland

Thomas Husted
American University

Takanobu Igarashi
Bankers Trust Company

Gerald Jones
Unisys Corporation

Donald W. Kiefer
Congressional Research Service

William Kitt
Eaton Corporation

Kenneth H. Klein
Xerox Corporation

Jerome Kurtz
Paul, Weiss, Rifkind, Wharton & Garrison

Rudi Kurz
Brookings Institution

Patrick J. Kusiak
Department of Defense

John F. Kyle
Exxon Corporation

Richard W. Lang
Federal Reserve Bank of Philadelphia

Donald C. Lubick
Hodgson, Russ, Andrews, Woods & Goodyear

Rosemary D. Marcuss
Congressional Budget Office

Robert A. McConnell
CBS, Inc.

Paul Moeller
Baltimore Gas and Electric Company

Wilbur Monroe
Monroe Associates

John Nelson
Port Authority of New York and New Jersey

Thomas S. Neubig
Department of the Treasury

Richard A. Overton
Monsanto Company

Ronald A. Pearlman
Bryan, Cave, McPheeters & McRoberts

Lewis L. Pearson
U.S. Fidelity and Guaranty

Joseph A. Pechman
Brookings Institution

Dean P. Phypers
International Business Machines Corporation

John Post
Brookings Institution

Robert W. Raynsford
Department of the Army

C. H. Reing
Mobil Oil Corporation

John F. Rolph
CitiBank

Stanford G. Ross
Arnold & Porter

Catherine Rudder
American Political Science Association

Samantha P. Sanchez
The Taxpayers' Committee

Frtiz Scheuren
Internal Revenue Service

Frank W. Schiff
Committee for Economic Development

Lee Sheppard
Tax Notes

Rosemarie L. Shomstein
Equitable Life Assurance Society

Delos R. Smith
The Conference Board

Eugene Steuerle
American Enterprise Institute for Public Policy Research

Gerard Strainchamps
Embassy of France

Laura Van Etten
Equitable Life Assurance Society

Charls E. Walker
Charls E. Walker Associates

Randall D. Weiss
Joint Committee on Taxation

John M. Yinger
Syracuse University

John Yurow
Arent, Fox, Kintner, Plotkin & Kahn